Target Score

SECOND EDITION

A communicative course for TOEIC® Test Preparation

Charles Talcott   Graham Tullis

Student's Book with two Audio CDs

TOEIC® is a registered trademark of Educational Testing Service (ETS).
This publication is not endorsed or approved by ETS.

CAMBRIDGE
UNIVERSITY PRESS

CAMBRIDGE UNIVERSITY PRESS
Cambridge, New York, Melbourne, Madrid, Cape Town,
Singapore, São Paulo, Delhi, Tokyo, Mexico City

Cambridge University Press
The Edinburgh Building, Cambridge CB2 8RU, UK

www.cambridge.org
Information on this title: www.cambridge.org/9780521706643

First edition published 2006
Second edition 2007
4th printing 2011

Cover design by Andrew Oliver
Design concept by Manor Farm Design
Page make-up by Hart McLeod

Printed in Dubai by Oriental Press

A catalogue record for this publication is available from the British Library

ISBN 978-0-521-70664-3 Student's Book
ISBN 978-0-521-70665-0 Teacher's Book

Authors' note

Put your English to the test with *Target Score*.

Target Score is a new coursebook specifically designed for people who want to improve their overall level in international English and measure their performance against an established benchmark: the new TOEIC® test – Test of English for International Communication.

This new edition of *Target Score* has been extensively revised and updated to reflect the changes that have been introduced on the redesigned TOEIC®. The core components of *Target Score* remain the same but now include new exercises, new recordings with a variety of accents and new test material to make sure that you can prepare successfully for the new TOEIC® test.

Target Score combines an active communicative approach to learning authentic international English with interactive, classroom-friendly TOEIC® preparation exercises and practice tests. The twelve units and the four review tests provide a comprehensive course that prepares you for the final practice test.

The authors, building on their experience teaching English in international companies, universities and business schools, have created an exciting and challenging course that focuses on the real international situations and settings featured on the new TOEIC®. Each of the units blends interesting authentic content with practical effective TOEIC® preparation exercises and tips.

With *Target Score* you'll be ready to achieve your top score on the TOEIC® and be able to use the language skills you've learned in your professional and personal life.

Enjoy the course!

Charles Talcott
Graham Tullis

Map of book

Viewpoint	Communication	TOEIC® Tips
Indian Companies Cultural training for employees	Preparing a job interview	• Forms of address • Wh- questions: *How* + adj / adv
Little Brother Surveillance in the workplace	Participating in a discussion	• Eye for photos • Prepositions of place / time • Skimming a text
Writing It Down or Talking It Up Cultures of communication	Holding a press conference	• Listening for keywords • Past time expressions
Camper A company profile	Making a product presentation	• Word stress: verbs / nouns • Answering tag questions
Robots To The Rescue Robots in Japan	Attending a meeting	• Antonyms • Looking for links • Listening for main ideas
Juan Valdez Developing the coffee market	Presenting arguments	• Verbs expressing the future • Words with more than one meaning
Norway's Coolest Movie Theater and Far Off Course Leisure and sport activities	Organizing a team event	• Homonyms and similar-sounding words • Participle forms as adjectives
Cashflow 101 Learning about finance	Buying and selling	• Abbreviations • Expressing figures
Exotic Trips For Eco-tourists New developments in tourism	Negotiating a contract	• Words ending in *-ly* • Words expressing condition
City Limits Urban planning for the future	Taking part in a discussion	• Partially true statements • *Say* and *tell*
Living The Longer Life The Okinawa lifestyle	Designing a company program	• Gerunds • Question forms: suggesting
To Kill An Avatar Virtual worlds	Participating in a debate	• Listening for details • Subjunctive

About the book

Target Score has twelve topic-based units and four review tests. After every three units, you can measure your progress with authentic TOEIC®-style questions in the review test section. When you finish all four review tests, you will have completed 200 TOEIC®-style questions.

A detailed description of the official TOEIC® is included on page 7. If you are not familiar with the TOEIC®, you should read this section before starting the course.

Each unit has been designed to create a balance between English language skills acquisition and TOEIC® practice with listening and reading exercises that are carefully matched to the seven parts on the TOEIC®. Icons like this ▲ appear next to the exercises to indicate which of the seven parts of the test the exercise is preparing you for.

Each unit contains the following components:

Snapshot
Listening
Grammar Check
Vocabulary Builder
Viewpoint
Communication
TOEIC® tips

Each unit opens with **Snapshot** which features four photographs illustrating topics covered in the unit. You will practice analyzing images through communicative activities or TOEIC®-style Part 1 listening exercises.

The two **Grammar Check** sections in each unit will help you review and consolidate the key elements of English grammar that are essential for effective communication in international English and success on the TOEIC®. These sections include TOEIC®-style incomplete sentences from Part 5 and text completion practice from Part 6. The grammar points are cross-referenced to the **Grammar Reference** section in the back of the coursebook on pages 129–137, which gives further explanations and examples of usage.

Each unit contains several **Listening** sections where you will develop your listening comprehension skills. Where you see you will hear a variety of TOEIC®-style listenings: Part 1 statements, Part 2 questions and responses, Part 3 short conversations, and Part 4 short talks.

The **Vocabulary Builder** section teaches you strategies for expanding your vocabulary, focusing on keywords and terms that are commonly used in everyday English and often included on the TOEIC®. Vocabulary Builder sections provide further practice in incomplete sentences and text completion for Parts 5 and 6 of the test.

Viewpoint presents authentic reading texts from a wide range of international sources and includes a variety of questions and activities to test your reading comprehension. The texts focus on contemporary issues and highlight topic areas featured on the TOEIC®. Discussion sections provide an opportunity for everyone to explore and express their own point of view while improving fluency.

The **Communication** section concludes each unit with a speaking activity such as a discussion, a negotiation, or a debate. This allows you to actively practice the English you've learned in each unit and gives you the chance to interact with others just as you would in the professional world.

Each unit contains two **TOEIC® tip** boxes, which give you strategies to adopt and practical advice about what to look out for when taking the test.

A practical **Wordlist** at the back of the book includes a selection of keywords from each unit that frequently appear on the TOEIC®. The **Answer Key** for the unit exercises and activities and the four review tests can be found at the back of the book on page 156. The complete **Audioscripts** for all of the listening sections begin on page 140.

Overview of the TOEIC® Test
Test of English for International Communication

What is the TOEIC®?

The TOEIC® is a test of international English that is taken every year by 4.5 million students and business professionals in different countries around the world.* The two-hour test includes 200 multiple-choice questions and is divided into two sections: Listening and Reading. There are 100 questions on each section.

Listening (45 minutes)
- Part 1 Picture identification
- Part 2 Question/Response
- Part 3 Short conversations
- Part 4 Short talks

Reading (1 hour 15 minutes)
- Part 5 Incomplete sentences
- Part 6 Text completion
- Part 7 Reading comprehension

You will find a description of each part of the test below, followed by a box with specific strategies that will help you to maximize your score.

*For more information consult the TOEIC® web page at www.toeic.com.

The Listening Test

This section of the test has four separate parts and lasts 45 minutes.

Part 1 Picture identification (10 questions)

In Part 1 you will see a selection of ten black-and-white photographs and you will hear a series of ten recordings. For each photo you will hear four descriptive statements. You must identify the one statement that best describes what you can see in the picture.

- Always look closely at each photo and ask yourself the following questions :
  Who is in the photo?
  What objects are visible?
  Where was the photo taken?
  What are the professions of the people?
  What actions are being performed?
  What are the positions of the people and the objects?
- Make sure that you listen to the complete statement. Some statements may only be partially true.
- Watch out for homonyms and similar-sounding words that have different meanings.

Part 2 Question/Response (30 questions)

Part 2 features 30 recordings of questions and responses. Each question is followed by three responses. You must select the appropriate response.

- The questions that you will hear will be of different types. Try to determine what type of question is being asked and what the purpose of the question is. Some questions ask for information but others may be invitations, suggestions or comments.
- Listen carefully to the beginning of the question, especially for question words such as *who, what, where*, etc.
- Do not expect the answer to a question to contain the same verb and tense as the question.

Part 3 Short conversations (30 questions)

Part 3 features ten four-part conversations between two people. After listening to each conversation, you have to answer three comprehension questions. Each question has four multiple-choice answers, only one of which is correct.

- Always read the questions before you hear the recording. This will help you to focus on what is said and you may even be able to guess the meaning of words that you do not understand.
- While you are listening to the conversation, try to identify who the speakers are, where the conversation takes place and what they are talking about.
- Listen for keywords that will help you to identify the context.

Part 4 Short talks (30 questions)

Part 4 presents ten recorded short talks that may include announcements, weather reports, travel advisories, etc. You must answer three comprehension questions about each talk. Each question has four multiple-choice answers, only one of which is correct.

- Read as many questions as you can before you hear the short talk – but do not read the answers. You will not have time and they will distract you.
- Focus on the introduction and the first part of the talk to determine the context.
- Memorize key information as you listen and do not try to answer any questions before you have listened to the whole talk.

The Reading Test

This section of the test has three parts and lasts one hour and fifteen minutes.

Part 5 Incomplete sentences (40 questions)

Part 5 consists of sentences that contain a blank. You are given four possible answers to complete the sentence. You must choose the correct one.

> - Ask yourself whether the question is testing vocabulary or a grammar point.
> - Analyze the sentence and try to identify the parts of speech – i.e. noun, adjective, etc. This will help you to choose the correct answer especially on vocabulary questions.
> - Figure out the meaning and/or the type of word by looking at prefixes and suffixes.
> - Look for grammatical relationships in the sentence, i.e. cause/effect, conditionals, verb tense agreement, etc.

Part 6 Text completion (12 questions)

Part 6 presents three texts which each contain four numbered blanks. You are given four possible answers to complete each blank. You must choose the correct one.

> - Scan the whole text to see how it is constructed.
> - Read the directions that are given for each text – this will tell you what types of documents are presented and may help you to select appropriate answers, especially in questions that focus on lexical items.
> - Read all of the questions carefully and ask yourself:
>   - if they require you to refer to information or arguments presented in different parts of the text in order to answer the questions;
>   - if they require you to analyze the grammatical structure of part of the document in order to determine the appropriate tense time or form of agreement, i.e. singular/plural, etc.

Part 7 Reading comprehension (48 questions)

In this section of the test, you must read several documents and answer multiple-choice questions about them. The documents are presented in two different formats:

Single passages These present individual documents (announcements, news articles, letters, invoices, timetables, etc.) and you must answer between two and four comprehension questions on each document by choosing the best answer.

Double passages These feature two documents which are inter-related. The first document presents information and is followed by a second document that contains a response, reaction or enquiry relating to the first one. You must answer five questions on each of the double passages.

There are 28 questions for the single passages and 20 for the double passages.

> - Skim the questions before reading in order to establish a focus for reading.
> - Be familiar with the layout of common types of texts such as emails, memos or formal letters in order to facilitate your reading.
> - Read the title and the first line of the text to determine what kind of text it is and identify the main idea.
> - Remember that an answer may require that you understand information in different parts of the text.
> - For the sections that feature double passages, you should read both documents in order to understand the relationship between the two. Remember that some questions will require you to cross-check information between the two documents. You should therefore allow more time for double passages.

General test-taking strategies

The following simple strategies can help you to perform better on the test:
- Bring a good quality pencil and eraser.
- Make sure that you are familiar with the instructions for each section of the test before you take it. That will help you to concentrate on the questions and you will be able to use your time more effectively.
- Do not panic if you hear or read words that you do not understand. Focusing on the general context will usually help you to answer correctly.
- Remember that you are not penalized for incorrect answers so always give an answer to each question.
- If you cannot find the right answer to a question in the Listening section or you have not understood part of the recording – do not panic! Choose an answer that you think is possible and move on to focus on the next question.
- Do not let yourself be distracted by a difficult question in the Listening section. You only have limited time between each question so you must answer quickly and be ready to listen to the next one.
- Make sure that you do not run out of time when doing the Reading section. Remember that your time is limited.
- Even if you do not have enough time to finish all the questions in the Reading section, you should still complete the answer grid by guessing.

1 Careers

Snapshot

1 Look at the pictures. Choose the situation that describes what is happening in each of them. What clues helped you to decide?

1 a board meeting   b general assembly   c contract negotiation
2 a company picnic   b workers' demonstration   c fire drill
3 a conference call   b job interview   c sales presentation
4 a retirement award   b press conference   c product demonstration

DISCUSSION

* When do people start work in your country?
* When do they retire?
* How do companies recruit?

Listening 1

Notes

1 Sabrina - check
availability!

2

3

 **A** Laura Alvarado is the manager of
PeoplePower, a temporary work agency.
Listen to three conversations that she has
with clients and write the keywords on the
notepad.

B Fill in the information in the table below.

	Name of caller	Subject of call	Action to be taken
Call 1			
Call 2			
Call 3	Laura Alvarado		

Grammar Check 1

Present simple and present continuous

We use the present simple:
a   to talk about things that happen regularly.
b   to express our thoughts and feelings.
c   to tell a story.
d   to talk about future events that have a timetable.

A   Read the sentences below and match them with the uses they illustrate.

1   Then she gets offered a job in this small town in the country. So, she decides to move there with the family.   ....
2   We usually start at 7:30 and work through until 4:00.   ....
3   I think they need to hire some extra staff.   ....
4   We fly back from Lisbon on Friday afternoon   ....

We use the present continuous:
a   to describe things that are happening as we speak.
b   to talk about changes that are taking place.
c   to refer to conditions that are temporary.
d   to talk about immediate future plans.

*Some verbs are not used in the continuous form.
● see page 129 in the Grammar Reference section

B   Read the sentences below and match them with the uses they illustrate.

1   Companies are using more temporary workers.   ....
2   The first candidate is arriving at nine.   ....
3   She's printing out some documents.   ....
4   I'm replacing him all this week.   ....

6   **C**   Read about the findings of a U.S. survey of the recruitment of college graduates and choose the correct verb tense.

NEWS BRIEF

PowerPeople announced that it ¹(*releases / is releasing*) its annual survey of how the world of work ²(*changes / is changing*). This year's survey ³(*examines / is examining*) how the new generation of workers that is entering the job market today ⁴(*compares / is comparing*) to their parents' generation, the baby boomers. The most recent findings ⁵(*show / are showing*) what these young professionals, fresh from college, are thinking as they move into the world of work. It ⁶(*appears / is appearing*) that a significant proportion (65%) of those interviewed ⁷(*expect / are expecting*) to have better job prospects than their parents. Their optimism, however, is not always shared by employers, and while the majority ⁸(*agrees / is agreeing*) that the new generation ⁹(*possesses / is possessing*) the technical skills that ¹⁰(*become / are becoming*) essential in the modern hi-tech work environment, they also ¹¹(*suggest / are suggesting*) that they ¹²(*do not have / are not having*) some of the other equally important skills, especially in communication.

Vocabulary Builder

A Professions Quiz. Look at the pictures of famous people who started out in very different jobs to the ones that made them famous. What professions made them famous? What did they do before?

1 Paul Gauguin

2 Charles Lindbergh

3 Alfred Hitchcock

4 Marilyn Monroe

5 Ralph Lauren

6 J K Rowling

7 Hillary Clinton

Suffixes

We can make new words by adding groups of letters to the end of a word. The following suffixes all designate people who do certain jobs, or share the same activities.

artist	photographer / editor
employee	cameraman / camerawoman
musician	applicant / president

B Match each group of words (1–6) with one of the suffixes above.

1 *-ist*	2	3	4	5	6 ....
public	optic	supervise	train	consult	fire
biology	electric	labor	refer	account	sales
pharmacy	statistic	design	trust	attend	repair
reception	history	survey	address	assist	crafts
economy	library	engine	interview	correspond	chair

 C Complete the sentences with appropriate words from the lists above.

1 We have called in a group of *consultants* to review our accounting procedures.
2 The .... of the board has announced that two new directors will be appointed next month.
3 The .... says it'll take him another hour to restore the power supply.
4 Most .... are predicting that domestic spending will pick up speed in the second half of the year.

Viewpoint

 Read the following questions before skimming the article to find the correct answers.

1 Why did Mr. Kumar and his colleagues attend the training session?
2 What do employees like Mr. Kumar most need to learn?
3 What should you NOT do when you meet an American for the first time?
4 What results have been obtained by training programs like these?

Indian Companies Are Adding Western Flavor

BY SARITHA RAI
New York Times August 19

Arun Kumar had never shaken hands with a foreigner nor needed to wear a necktie. He vaguely thought that raising a toast had something to do with eating bread. But Mr. Kumar, 27, and six other engineers were recently recruited by the Hyderabad offices of Sierra Atlantic, a software company based in Fremont, Calif. And before they came face-to-face with American customers, the new employees went through a challenging four-week training session aimed at providing them with global-employee skills like learning how to speak on a conference call and how to address colleagues.

As more and more service jobs migrate to India, such training programs are increasingly common. Sierra Atlantic says that one-fourth of its 400 employees working out of the Hyderabad offices are constantly interacting with foreigners.

For Sierra and others, the training in Western ways is intended not only to help employees perform daily business interactions with American or European colleagues and customers but also to help the companies transcend their image as cheap labor.

"Your interaction with people of other cultures will only increase," Colonel Gowri Shankar, Sierra's trainer, told Mr. Kumar and half a dozen other young engineers, "and you should be equally at ease whether in Hyderabad or Houston." The Sierra programmers listened attentively as Colonel Shankar listed common complaints: speaking one of India's many languages in front of foreigners, questioning colleagues about their compensation, and cracking ethnic jokes. He is uncompromising on punctuality and protocol. "Americans are friendly, but do not slap an American on his back or call him by his first name in the first meeting," said Colonel Shankar.

Some companies are already seeing the benefits of the training. Sierra said that in February, its Indian unit won a bid against an Indian competitor because the Sierra employees were seen as a better fit. "It all adds up to better rates and bigger projects," said the project leader, Kalyani Manda.

⚠ TOEIC® Tip

Pay attention to forms of address. They give helpful clues about the context.

- First names for informal situations.
- *Mr., Miss, Mrs.,* or *Ms.* before last names for formal situations (i.e. with clients or customers).
- *Sir* or *Madam*, which are very formal, to address customers (i.e. restaurant or hotel guests).

DISCUSSION

What is your reaction to the article?
Do you think Sierra Atlantic's training policy for its Indian employees is a good example of how to motivate and train staff?
How would you feel if you had to change your style of dress or behavior to suit the business culture of a foreign employer?

"So, Jim, where do you see yourself in ten minutes?"

Grammar Check 2

Wh- questions

Questions that begin with "**wh-** question forms" such as *who*, *what*, *where*, and *how* ask for information about:

a people	c time	e duration
b things	d places	f manner

 see page 129 in the Grammar Reference section

A Look at the questions. What kind of information do they refer to?

1 When was the last time you were interviewed?   c
2 Who interviewed you?   ....
3 What questions did the interviewer ask?   ....
4 How long did the interview last?   ....
5 Where did the interview take place?   ....
6 How did you feel about the interview afterwards?   ....

B Complete the personal information questions on the form with the correct question word.

HR Department		
	1 ...*Where*...	were you born?
	2	did you graduate from high school?
Employee Background Information	3	children do you have?
	4	languages are you fluent in?
	5	do you live with?
	6	do you weigh?
	7	social organizations do you belong to?
	8	old are you?

⚠ TOEIC® Tip

Listen carefully to the first words of questions in Part 2 of the test.

How followed by an adjective or an adverb gives the question a very specific focus.

- *How* + adjective (size or degree)
  How tall are you? How qualified is he? How experienced are they?

- *How* + adverb (frequency and duration)
  How often do you speak a foreign language? How long does a job interview usually last?

In the United States, there are laws regulating what types of questions a recruiter can ask. Which of the questions above do you think are illegal in the U.S.?

DISCUSSION

What questions should a recruiter NOT be allowed to ask?
What interview questions are illegal in your country?
Are men and women asked the same questions in interviews? If not, is this fair? Is this legal?

Listening 2

 2 Read the following responses given during a job interview. What questions do you think the interviewer asked? Now listen to the interviewer's questions (A–G) and match them with the correct response. Be careful, two questions are not answered!

1 .... A
> The ideal supervisor has strong leadership skills. She or he inspires all members of the team to strive for maximum results.

2 ....
> Well, I enjoy team sports. I'm captain of a soccer team. I also like playing chess and participate in amateur tournaments.

3 ....
> Currently I head a team of eight people. I manage their schedules, oversee their results and conduct training seminars.

4 ....
> Since I was promoted to international sales, I've been working hard on my foreign languages.

5 ....
> I'm highly motivated and dedicated to improving both my personal performance and that of the company. I get a lot of satisfaction out of seeing a group of people achieve a common goal.

Which two questions have not been answered? Write out the questions.

Listening 3

7 A Read the following flyer and find two expressions that refer to:

1 people who hire staff ....
2 people who are looking for employment ....
3 recruitment methods ....

Don't miss the tenth annual Eastern States Job Fair

MAY 14–15

Welcome human resources professionals, recruiters, and job-seekers to the largest job fair in the country. This year's fair promises to be one of the best ever.

Over 300 booths presenting the latest recruitment trends, the hottest hiring tools and the sharpest interviewing strategies for both headhunters and job-hunters.

Hundreds of major companies will be conducting on-site interviews!

50 seminars and workshops, from e-recruiting to successful résumé writing.

The Eastern States Trade Show Plaza

  4 B You're attending the Eastern States Job Fair. Listen to extracts from the two talks and correct the six errors on the Job Fair program.

Eastern States Job Fair		
Seminars and Workshops	Speaker:	**Don Stanley** IS
Saturday May 17	Seminar Title:	"Getting the most out of the ~~50~~-minute interview"
Morning Sessions	Summary:	Interviews should be longer and more efficient.
	Time:	9:00 a.m. in Seminar Room 32
		This seminar is of special interest to interviewees.
	Speaker:	**Kimberly Armstrong**
	Workshop Title:	"Taking full advantage of job advertisements"
	Summary:	Interviewers also need to learn what questions to ask.
	Time:	11:00 a.m. in Workshop Room 47
		This workshop is of special interest to recruiters.

Communication

Temporary work agency interviews

PeoplePower is one of the fastest growing temporary work agencies in the area and represents the best and the brightest executives, skilled professionals, and craftspeople in a wide range of jobs. They are currently expanding their listings and have arranged interviews with top candidates.

Choose whether you would like to be a co-director of PeoplePower or one of the candidates and consult your role cards on page 168.

2 Workplaces

Snapshot

1

2

3

4

⚠ TOEIC® Tip

Develop an eye for photos in Part 1 of the test.
Practice putting words to images. First, quickly scan the photos. What English words come to mind? Ask: *Who … is doing … what*? Identify the people. Describe the actions. Name the objects.

A Look at the pictures and name the objects you see in each picture. Then identify the workplaces and the jobs associated with them.

B Now make two statements describing each picture.

DISCUSSION

What different places have you worked in?
What did you like / dislike about these places?

Grammar Check 1

Count and non-count nouns

a   Nouns which have both singular and plural forms are count nouns.
b   Nouns which have no plural form and which are never preceded by the indefinite article *a* or *an* are non-count nouns.

● see page 130 in the Grammar Reference section

A   In the paragraph below, five nouns have been <u>underlined</u>. Which category, a or b, do they belong to?

BlueSpace

Imagine an ¹<u>office</u> equipped with embedded ²<u>software</u> that instantly responds to your arrival by adjusting its temperature, lighting and airflow to your preferred settings. It then unlocks sealed ³<u>information</u> on your ⁴<u>computer</u> and then, with overhead lights, announces your ⁵<u>presence</u> to your colleagues.

1 ....*a*....   2 ....   3 ....   4 ....   5 ....

   B   Complete the text below, adding the appropriate nouns from the box. You should give plural forms where necessary.

| researcher | architecture | furniture | work | person |
| team | ~~result~~ | impact | privacy | transition |

Bluespace is the ¹....*result*.... of a unique venture between the IBM corporation and Steelcase, a U.S. company that specializes in the design and ².................. of office spaces. Together they have explored the potential for combining office ³.................. and microprocessors to create an intelligent workspace. ⁴.................. at the Bluespace project believe that changes in the nature of ⁵.................. require new solutions and they aim to create an office space which takes account of the ⁶.................. of new information technologies. Today employees do different kinds of work during office hours; sometimes they may need total ⁷.................. but at other moments they may need to work collaboratively in ⁸................... And the objective of Bluespace is to allow a smooth ⁹.................. between the two environments. As Mark Grenier, vice president of the research department, says, "With Bluespace we're discovering new ways of providing ¹⁰.................. with flexibility and control of their workspace."

Listening 1

A Look at the following selection of complaints from a survey of office working conditions. Which three would you find the most annoying? Discuss your answers with a partner.

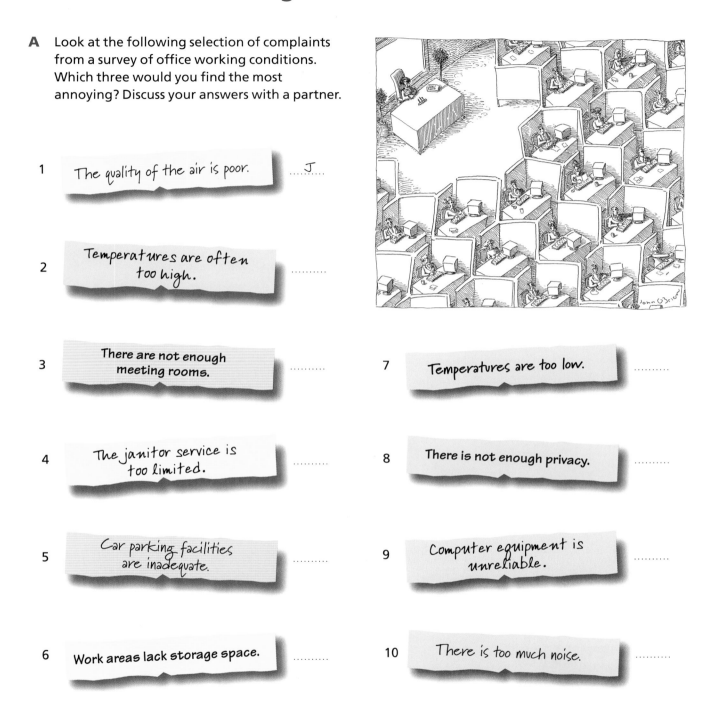

1 The quality of the air is poor.   ....J....

2 Temperatures are often too high.   ....

3 There are not enough meeting rooms.   ....

4 The janitor service is too limited.   ....

5 Car parking facilities are inadequate.   ....

6 Work areas lack storage space.   ....

7 Temperatures are too low.   ....

8 There is not enough privacy.   ....

9 Computer equipment is unreliable.   ....

10 There is too much noise.   ....

B Listen to ten questions (A–J). Which complaint does each one refer to? Write your answers in the spaces provided above.

Grammar Check 2

Prepositions of place

● see page 130 in the Grammar Reference section

A Prepositions help us to describe where things are. Look at the illustrations and complete each sentence with the appropriate preposition from the box.

above	through	toward(s)	under
~~around~~	alongside	against	opposite
within	along		

1 The chairs are arranged ...*around*... the table.
2 The two people are sitting .... each other.
3 The woman is cycling .... the pathway.
4 The truck is parked .... the motorcycle.
5 The bus is driving .... the bridge.
6 The man is watching the race .... his binoculars.
7 The women are walking .... the exit.
8 No one is allowed .... the perimeter fence.
9 There is a sign .... the door.
10 The ladder is leaning .... the wall.

B In which of the sentences (1–9) above could the following prepositions also be used?

inside	...*8*...	beneath	....	with	....
beside	....	down	....	to	....
round	....	across from	....	over	....

C Choose the preposition that best completes the following sentences.

1 The employee lounge is located on the third floor just .... the water cooler.
   a towards   b around   c through   d opposite
2 In the event of a power failure employees should remain .... their offices until advised that it is safe for them to leave.
   a alongside   b beside   c inside   d round
3 Turn left, walk .... to the end of the corridor, my office is the last one on the right.
   a over   b against   c through   d down
4 The fire door leads .... an emergency staircase.
   a to   b beneath   c over   d with
5 The underground parking lot has two levels. The top one is reserved for staff but visitors can use the one .... it.
   a above   b along   c beside   d below
6 Instructions on emergency procedures are posted at eye level .... the elevator door.
   a under   b beside   c within   d round

⚠ TOEIC® Tip

Watch out for preposition forms that refer to both place and time.
*It took them **over** two hours to install.*
*We should be arriving **around** five.*
*Royalties are not payable **beyond** the period of the agreement.*
Here are some others:
before   to   from
by   under   after

Listening 2

A Make a list of the objects that you would find in an office for each of the following categories.

1 paperwork: ....*faxes, envelopes*....
2 publications: ....
3 office supplies: ....
4 electrical equipment: ....
5 personal items: ....

B Look at the picture of Alison's office. Which of the objects can you see?

C Listen to Alison describing her office. Where does she keep the following things?

1 invoices: ....*in-box tray*....
2 price lists: ....
3 personal items: ....
4 customer files: ....
5 printer cartridges: ....

ACTIVE PRACTICE

Work with a partner. **Student A** should refer to the picture of the office on page 168 and **Student B** to the picture on page 169. Not all of the items are in the same positions in both pictures. Describe where the objects are in your picture using prepositions of place. How many differences can you find?

Vocabulary Builder

Word families

Some families of words include the same one-syllable root form. When prefixes are added to the beginning and / or suffixes to the end of such words, they take on different meanings. Complete the diagram for the word *form* by:

A adding prefixes and suffixes from the box to circles 1–6.

B adding combinations of both prefixes and suffixes to circle 7.

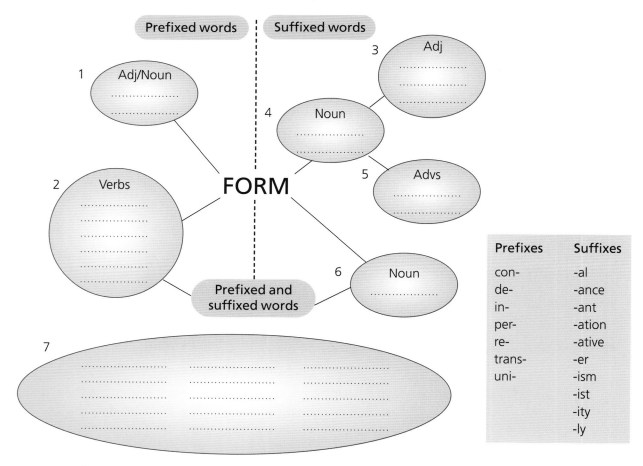

C Complete the sentences with a word from the completed diagram in an appropriate form.

1   Dr. Vincenzo is the ....*former*.... Vice President of our local Chamber of Commerce.
2   Participants in the gala evening are reminded that they must wear .... dress.
3   The cabin crew will be issued with new .... next month.
4   Application .... can be downloaded directly from our website.
5   Our .... in meeting key market targets has been disappointing.

D Choose one of the words below and use a dictionary to make a word family diagram.

draw   present   quest   sign   move   employ

Viewpoint

 A What does the title tell you about the article? Read the first sentence. What additional information do the keywords give you about the content of the text?

Little Brother sees into your cubicle

By Joan Fleischer Tamen
South Florida Sun-Sentinel

The next time you log on at work, the boss could be gathering data to see what you've been up to.

Computer technology can document, analyze, measure, and monitor almost every aspect of an employee's performance. It can count keystrokes per minute, as well as clock your workday like a punch card. It can track distractions such as time spent at an eBay auction or a naughty cyber site.

Software can even show managers what employees are saying over instant messages, or how much time they're spending on the phone.

In Florida, a secretary was fired this year after bosses cited "excessive personal use of company equipment."

Her employer had installed software that monitored outgoing phone calls and recorded the phone numbers, call durations, and to whom they were placed. The secretary had made 300 personal calls during a three-month period, according to the plaintiff's attorney, who won the case and obtained unemployment benefits for her client.

With studies showing that the average worker spends 75 minutes a day surfing the Internet, and with managers pressured to squeeze more out of their staffs, using technology to monitor employees is big business.

A survey on employee surveillance found that three-fourths of major U.S. firms record and review their workers' communications. And about half of companies polled said they had fired or disciplined employees for violating the company's computer policies.

Miami lawyer Mark Cheskin says he has used computer records to defeat an employee who sued for overtime pay. "Someone can claim they're working 12-hour days, but an electronic record can track tardiness, your coming and going, and when you're at your desk," said Cheskin.

Inexpensive technology is spurring the growth of employee monitoring, according to the Privacy Foundation in Denver. Critics such as Frederick Lane, attorney and author, say most workers would be shocked to know how vulnerable they are.

"It really raises the question of the relationship between employer and employee," said Lane. "Does the information that the company can gather outweigh the psychological impact on the employee who feels they can never take a break because a whole host of 'Little Brothers' are watching?"

B Now read the whole article and choose the best answer to the following questions.

1 Why was the Florida secretary dismissed?
   a She made personal telephone calls.
   b She visited too many websites.
   c She spent too much time away from her desk.
2 What percentage of major U.S. firms monitor employee communications?
   a 75 % b 50% c 12%
3 The market for employee monitoring software is expected to grow because:
   a employees are less productive.
   b the Internet is expanding.
   c surveillance software is cheaper than before.

DISCUSSION

Does the use of high-tech surveillance equipment violate an individual's right to privacy? What are the potential abuses of surveillance technology?

Listening 3

When people communicate in the workplace, most of the time they are talking about things that are directly connected to their jobs. The list in A below gives some examples of this type of communication.

A Complete the list using an appropriate verb from the box below.

~~request~~ review discuss suggest assign issue express

1 ...*request*... information
2 .... instructions
3 .... tasks
4 .... performance
5 .... changes
6 .... opinions
7 .... problems

  B Now listen to three short conversations (A–C) between employees. Which of the items above (1–7) do they illustrate? Write the letter (A–C) next to the correct item.

---

the Franklin Institute

Worried about Campus Security?

Voice your concerns at an information session on video surveillance.

Tuesday, Oct. 10 at 7:00 p.m.

BRADLEY CONFERENCE ROOM

Communication

Safety screening

The Franklin Institute provides technical education and training to students and professionals. Recently there have been a number of security incidents involving theft of equipment and personal belongings and unauthorized entry. As a result the Institute is now reviewing security procedures and is considering installing a closed circuit video surveillance system. An information session has been organized to address the question of whether or not video surveillance should be introduced.

Choose one of the role cards on pages 168–169 to help you prepare for the meeting.

3 Communications

Snapshot

A   Choose one photo and write five words that describe the people, actions, and objects in it. Using words from your list, write one statement for the photo.

B   Now listen to the statements (A–H) and select two that describe each picture.

Vocabulary Builder

Compound nouns (noun + noun)

Compound nouns are common word combinations, such as *magazine subscription*, *home page*, and *directory assistance*. The first noun gives information about the second noun.

A	B
voice	page
cable	bulletin
mail	mail
post	box
feature	booth
phone	television
front	browser
computer	article
news	screen
web	office

A Match the words in column A with those in column B to form compound nouns frequently used in the field of communications.

B Group the compound nouns into the correct categories.

Broadcasting	Press	Information Technology	Telecommunications	Postal Services
			voice mail	

C Complete the sentences with compound nouns from the exercises above.

1 Nobody was there when I called, so I left a message on your ....*voice mail*.........
2 Our company was profiled in a .... that appeared on the .... of today's paper.
3 If a package doesn't fit in your ...., then you usually have to pick it up at the ....

D How many compound nouns can you make with the words: *press*, *phone*, *news*?

Look for common word combinations as you get ready to take the TOEIC®!

Listening 1

A You will hear five short conversations (1–5) between two people. Fill in the boxes below.

	Who?	Where?	What?
1	customer and news agent		
2		at an airport	
3			sending a contract by fax or mail
4			
5			

B What keywords help you identify *who*, *where*, and *what* in each conversation?

Grammar Check 1

Articles *a, an, the*

A Read the following sentence and answer the questions below.

> Television is such *an* attractive and influential medium that *the* aboriginal communities in many parts of *the* world have set up *a* cooperative broadcasting network to preserve *the* local language and foster *the* native culture.

 see page 130 in the Grammar Reference section

1 Which articles are used with singular nouns?
2 Which article is used with plural nouns?
3 Which articles refer to something indefinite?
4 Which refer to something definite and specific?
5 Which noun does not have an article? Why?

6 B Read the text below and fill in the blanks with the appropriate article when needed.

Aboriginal Peoples
Television Network

¹...**The**.... launch of ²............ Aboriginal Peoples Television Network, or APTN, represents ³............ significant milestone for Aboriginal Canada. For ⁴............ first time in broadcast history, First Nations, Inuit and Metis people have ⁵............ opportunity to share their stories with ⁶............ rest of ⁷............ world on ⁸............ national television network dedicated to ⁹............ Aboriginal programming. Through ¹⁰............ documentaries, news, entertainment specials, and education programs, APTN offers ¹¹............ window onto¹²............ remarkably diverse worlds of Indigenous peoples in ¹³............ Canada and throughout ¹⁴............ world.

Viewpoint

Which do you prefer – exchanging emails or talking on the phone? Why?

 Read the newspaper article and answer the following questions.

1 What different types of communication are mentioned in the article?
2 Why do some cultures prefer written agreements to oral agreements?
3 What example is given of a "misuse" of communications technology?

"Got your email, thanks."

Writing it down or talking it up?
Contemporary "cultures of communication"

Whether local or global, private or professional, many communities rely on both oral and written forms of communication. But what carries greater weight: a piece of paper, a signature, someone's word, or a symbolic handshake? As cultures vary immensely, so do their preferred modes of communication.

Communities often favor oral or written modes of information exchange depending on their "culture of communication" and the type of exchange. But what form of communication remains more popular – speaking or writing?

In most Western cultures, a written contract is considered more binding than an oral agreement between individuals. The French, for example, tend to base legal decisions on written records because they are considered to be more reliable than spoken accounts.

The millions of cell phones sold every year might suggest that people prefer speaking to writing. On the other hand, many cell phone users send text messages rather than calling. "Texts are fun and more direct," says Ingrid Bergsen, "so my friends and I spend a lot less time talking on the phone and save on the monthly bill!"

The Internet has led to a dramatic rise in writing, from emails and bulletin-board postings to real-time chat lines, which are in fact a contemporary blend of oral and written exchange. But could it be that people are writing more and talking less? "I find myself sending quick emails to colleagues who work just down the hall to see if they want to go to lunch. We used to pick up the phone. Now everyone communicates everything over the net," recounts Sanjay Singh, a program developer in Silicon Valley.

Indeed some experts, such as corporate communications consultant Patsy Sander, have expressed concerns about the growing number of "misuses" of communication technology. According to Sander, "very important information that significantly impacts people's lives is being transmitted in ways that do not respect the codes and values of traditional information channels." Recently a large company in Great Britain informed its employees of massive layoffs by sending a text message over their cell phones. Imagine receiving the text message:

U R fired. Call hd'q.

Although the use of email and cell phones is efficient and convenient, Sander argues that "they risk breaking the fundamental bonds of trust that determine the richness of a community's information exchange. Sad to say, but some people forget that all communication starts with community."

DISCUSSION

1 What other ways of communicating are NOT mentioned in the article?
2 How would you describe your "culture of communication"? Is it primarily written or oral?
3 In your opinion, have people become too dependent on new forms of communication technology?
4 Can you think of any "misuses" of communications technology?

Listening 2

Telephoning

A The following questions are often heard during telephone conversations. Which ones would a caller ask? Which ones would the person receiving the call ask? How would you respond to the questions?

1   Can I have him call you back?   ....
2   How may I direct your call?   ....
3   Could you put me through to customer service?   ....
4   Would you like to leave a message?   ....
5   Do you know where she can be reached?   ....
6   Directory assistance. How may I help you?   ....
7   How do I get an outside line?   ....
8   Would you mind if I put you on loudspeaker?   ....
9   Is this extension 718?   ....
10 Would you happen to know when she'll be back in her office?   ....

 B Now listen to responses (A–J) and match them with questions (1–10).

C Use the following phrases to make more telephone questions.

Can I ...?   Would you happen to know ...?
Could I ...?   Do you know ...?
Would you like to ...?   What's your ...?
Would you like me to ...?   How may I ...?
Would you mind ...?   How do I ...?

ACTIVE PRACTICE

Quick caller

With a partner, challenge each other to respond as quickly as possible to the telephone questions above. As soon as your partner has responded to five questions, switch roles.

Grammar Check 2

Present perfect and past simple

A Look at the sentences and answer the questions.

> I *have had* this computer for three years.
> This year we *have purchased* five new laptop computers.
> I *purchased* a new computer last month.

1 Which tense is formed:
  – by adding *-ed* to the verb?
  – with the verb *have* + the past participle?
2 Which tense refers to:
  – an action that was finished in the past?
  – an action that started in the past but continues to the present?
  – a completed action that occurred during a period of time that continues to the present?

see page 131 in the Grammar Reference section

 B **Read the conversation between an Internet hotline technician and a customer, and choose the correct verb tense.**

Technician: Hello, MooseNet Hotline. How may I help you? ✓
Caller: Hello, I am phoning because lately we ¹(*have had* / *had*) a lot of problems with our Internet connections.
Technician: OK. May I first have your name, please?
Caller: Certainly. We ²(*have opened* / *opened*) the account last year in January under the name of Hank Williams Unlimited.
Technician: Here we are. Let me just confirm your account details. Are you still located at 1310 Lexington Avenue?
Caller: No. The company ³(*has moved* / *moved*) since opening the account. Last month we ⁴(*have relocated* / *relocated*) to 65 El Camino in Fresno.
Technician: So, what seems to be the problem?
Caller: Well, about four weeks ago, we ⁵(*have updated* / *updated*) our operating systems. Since then our Internet connection speeds ⁶(*have slowed* / *slowed*) down significantly.
Technician: Last month when you ⁷(*have changed* / *changed*) systems, ⁸(*have you switched* / *did you switch*) to a newer web browser?
Caller: No, we ⁹(*didn't* / *haven't*).
Technician: Since you ¹⁰(*have upgraded* / *upgraded*) your system last month, an older version of your browser must be causing the problem. Try installing a new version. If that doesn't work, call me back. We're available 24/7.

DISCUSSION

Work with a partner and interview each other about using computers.
Have you ever had problems with a computer?
What was the trouble? What did you do?
Have you ever called a hotline for help?
Have you ever checked a FAQ's (Frequently Asked Questions) web page for help?

> ⚠️ **TOEIC® Tip**
>
> In Parts 5 and 6 of the test, look for time expressions that help you decide which verb tense is correct.
> I *stopped* sending letters by mail five years *ago*.
> She *sent* them an email *yesterday*.
> We *have published* a company newsletter *since* 1995.
> *Lately* we *have done* most of our business over the phone.

ACTIVE PRACTICE

A Conduct the following Media Survey by asking another student the questions and recording his or her responses.

the Media Survey

1 What's your favorite information source? Why?
- ☐ Television
- ☐ Newspapers
- ☐ Magazines
- ☐ Radio
- ☐ Internet

2 Which types of information interest you the most?
- ☐ International news
- ☐ National news
- ☐ Local news
- ☐ Politics
- ☐ Editorials
- ☐ Business and finance
- ☐ Sports
- ☐ Arts and entertainment
- ☐ People

3 What types of audiovisual programs do you follow?
- ☐ News
- ☐ Documentaries
- ☐ Talk shows
- ☐ Comedy shows
- ☐ Soap operas
- ☐ Music
- ☐ Sports
- ☐ Educational

4 How often do you follow the news?
- ☐ Every day
- ☐ Every other day
- ☐ Occasionally
- ☐ Once a week
- ☐ Hardly ever
- ☐ Never

5 What do you use the Internet for?
- ☐ Instant messaging and chatting
- ☐ Downloading music
- ☐ Watching videos
- ☐ Emailing
- ☐ Maintaining your website
- ☐ Blogging
- ☐ Listening to podcasts
- ☐ Buying and selling online
- ☐ Playing games

B Share the responses with the rest of the class and discuss the results.

Listening 3

 4 Listen to the radio news bulletin about GloTelCom and answer the following questions.

1 What is GloTelCom going to do today?
2 What did GloTelCom do two months ago?
3 What are the job prospects for workers seeking employment in the area?
4 What have most large telecommunications companies already done?

Communication

Press conference: corporate layoffs

GloTelCom is going to hold a press conference to announce its plans to downsize. First the GloTelCom president and the spokesperson will make their statements. Then the mayor will give a brief speech. Next, the journalist and union representative will ask questions and present their arguments.

Decide which role you would like to play in the press conference and then read your role card on page 169.

Units 1–3

🎧 Listening Test

Part 1

Directions: Listen to the four recorded statements for each picture. Choose the statement that best describes what you see in the picture.

1

2

3

4

Part 2

Directions: You will hear nine recorded questions each followed by three responses. Choose the best response for each question.

5	A	B	C
6	A	B	C
7	A	B	C
8	A	B	C
9	A	B	C
10	A	B	C
11	A	B	C
12	A	B	C
13	A	B	C

Part 3

Directions: Listen to the two conversations and answer the three questions that are asked about each conversation.

14 What do the speakers usually do on Fridays?
- A Visit clients
- B Organize training events
- C Work from home
- D Make presentations

15 How do the man and woman feel?
- A Excited
- B Disappointed
- C Tired
- D Bored

16 What will the workshop be about?
- A Customer relations
- B Personnel management
- C Presentations
- D Time management

17 Who is collecting the money for the gift?
- A Steve
- B Dr. Camara
- C Anita
- D The research team

18 What is Dr. Camara going to do?
- A Make a donation
- B Retire
- C Transfer to a new job
- D Present an award

19 In which department does the woman work?
- A In accounting
- B In human resources
- C In finance
- D In research

Part 4

Directions: Listen to the two short talks and answer three questions on each.

20 Who does Ms. Jackson probably work for?
- A The postal service
- B The phone company
- C A business news publisher
- D A clothing store

21 Why is Ms. Jackson leaving a message?
- A To check a subscriber's address
- B To apologize to a subscriber for overcharging his account
- C To sell a new subscription
- D To inform a subscriber of a special offer

22 Which of the following is NOT true?
- A The subscription department does not have the full address
- B The subscriber has not paid his bill
- C The customer has not received *Business News*
- D The postal service cannot deliver the magazines

23 What is the purpose of the event?
- A To congratulate the new homeowners
- B To promote a new parking facility
- C To inaugurate a new real estate development
- D To break ground for the construction of a new park

24 Where does the event take place?
- A Downtown
- B At a performing arts center
- C At a state park
- D At an office complex

25 What facilities are provided to tenants?
- A Convenient warehouse storage
- B Full-service campus housing
- C The latest communications technology
- D Full insurance coverage

Reading Test

Part 5

Directions: Choose the one word or phrase that best completes the sentence.

26 The overseas reporter .... the editor yesterday.
A   is calling
B   has called
C   calls
D   called

27 The largest e-commerce company has just held a major press ....
A   conference
B   pass
C   release
D   office

28 The price lists are kept in the filing cabinet .... the photocopier.
A   along
B   beside
C   through
D   toward

29 The personnel director has .... department managers of the new hiring policies.
A   reformed
B   informed
C   performed
D   transformed

30 The offices are located .... the fourth floor of the Piazza building.
A   on
B   over
C   in
D   at

31 Currently Ms. Alonso .... the performance assessment plan for middle managers.
A   revise
B   is revising
C   has revised
D   revised

32 We need to purchase .... new office furniture.
A   a
B   many
C   several
D   some

33 Mr. Kim worked as an .... before launching his own company.
A   account
B   accountable
C   accountant
D   accounting

34 The top candidate will be offered .... exciting and lucrative career position.
A   a
B   an
C   each
D   other

35 Ms. Lee is going to the .... office to pick up a registered letter.
A   mail
B   package
C   post
D   stamp

36 Janet Foster, who was .... the president of the Riverside Corporation, has agreed to make the opening speech at the annual conference.
A   former
B   formal
C   formerly
D   formally

37 According to the latest news .... on KBCD radio, all traffic on the Pacoma Straits Bridge has been suspended due to gale-force winds.
A   agent
B   publication
C   bulletin
D   letter

Part 6

Directions: Four words or phrases are missing in the text. Choose the best answer to complete each empty space in the text.

Questions 38–41 refer to the following email.

Dear Colleagues,

I regret to inform you that, from November 1st, Pedro Esposito will be leaving his current ....

38 A   retirement
B   condition
C   location
D   position

as Area Marketing manager for Northern Europe.
I know that this has not been an easy decision for him but he .... that this is the right moment

39 A   has believed
B   believe
C   is believing
D   believes

for him to accept a new challenge in another field of activity. The two years that he has spent working with us have been extremely rewarding ones and we can all be very proud of the way our company has .... in an increasingly competitive marketplace.

40 A   conformed
B   reformed
C   performed
D   informed

Winning the health industry marketing award for the second time is a fitting tribute to both his leadership .... and to the quality of the team that worked with him.

41 A   tasks
B   skills
C   assignments
D   schedules

David Haskoff will be taking over from Pedro at the end of this month and I would be very grateful if you could attend the informal meeting that I have organized on Wednesday October 20th which will give me the opportunity to introduce him to you all.

Yours sincerely,
Cameron Carson, CEO.

Part 7

Directions: Read the following texts and choose the one best answer to each question.

Questions 42–44 refer to the following advertisement.

TOP ASSETS
Personnel Services

The right time, the right place, the right people.

For temporary or full-time banking personnel, count on Top Assets to provide highly-qualified, expertly trained people for a wide variety of positions. Tellers, customer service representatives, accounting clerks, loan processors, e-banking reps – we ensure the right people for the right places in your work environment. Top Assets personnel pass a comprehensive 18-step evaluation process and come with all the necessary credentials and experience. Call us today for a complimentary assessment of your bank's personnel needs.

Top Assets Personnel Services

Proud to provide the best people for the best businesses.

737-2895

www.top.assets.personnel.com

42 What kind of business is Top Assets?
A   An investment bank
B   A loan collection agency
C   An Internet service provider
D   An employment agency

43   What must a person have in order to work for Top Assets?
A   Insurance and references
B   A flexible schedule
C   Training and experience
D   The right work environment

44 What is Top Assets offering prospective clients?
A   A free evaluation
B   Eighteen days of free service
C   Financial insurance
D   A compliment

Questions 45–46 refer to the following advertisement.

International cellphone calls to all your friends for only one euro a week!

HOW FRIENDS.TEL WORKS

You call your friend overseas from your cellphone using a local Friends.Tel number and Friends.Tel connects you over the Internet.

First Create a Friends.Tel account.
   Sign up online and you'll receive a Friends.Tel phone number by email (and by SMS text message) to set up your account.

Second Credit your account.
   Pay the weekly one euro user fee by credit card online.

Third Create a Friends List.
   Enter the phone numbers of your friends who live abroad into the Friends List page. Each international number will be given a local Friends.Tel number that you dial when calling your friends.

Fourth Start calling.

Dial the number for your friend on your cellphone using the local Friends.Tel number and you're connected. You are only making and paying for a local call, but you will be connected internationally to your friend over the Internet.

45 What is offered by this service?
A   Inexpensive local calls
B   Inexpensive cell phones
C   Inexpensive international calls
D   Faster Internet connections

46 How does Friends.Tel communicate phone numbers to users?
A   By phone
B   By email and letter
C   By phone and fax
D   By email and text message

Questions 47–50 refer to the following article from a business magazine.

Is the energy flowing in your work space?

According to Lily Wong-Taylor, the director of the East / West Design Group, people don't think enough about the design dynamics of their work environment.

Her company develops office plans based on *feng shui*, an ancient Chinese earth science and ecological art form.

"Our primary goal is to produce a space that gathers, generates, and focuses natural energies that enable people to perform at their best," says Wong-Taylor. The group has worked with both small businesses and major architectural firms on large-scale commercial buildings and projects.

The group's design consultants first conduct an on-site assessment of the kind of energy that a company wants for the kinds of activities and work that need to be done. The work activities are then divided according to *feng shui* energy categories: fire, earth, water, wood, and metal. These elements determine the building materials and architectural features needed for an effective, harmonious workplace. The *feng shui* designer may also recommend landscaping, gardens, plant arrangements, and water elements. "You'd be surprised," says Wong-Taylor, "how the smallest water feature in an office space can generate a tremendous flow of productive energies."

47 What is the main activity of the East / West Design Group?
   A Producing fashion items
   B Selling office supplies
   C Environmental protection
   D Designing offices

48 How does the author of the article define *feng shui*?
   A As an ancient architectural site in China
   B As a commercial building project
   C As a traditional Asian practice of spatial arrangement
   D As a new type of design firm

49 According to the article, why would a company hire a *feng shui* consultant?
   A To improve cash flow
   B To increase productivity
   C To produce building materials
   D To reduce energy costs

50 When working with a new client, what does the East / West Design Group do first?
   A Conducts an online survey
   B Visits the company to evaluate its needs
   C Assesses the company's financial records
   D Recommends specific water features

4 Retailing

Snapshot

A   Look at the four pictures. What are the people doing?

1

2

3

4

 ⚠ TOEIC® Tip

Word stress

Many words in English can be both verbs and nouns, and are usually pronounced in the same way, such as *to market* (v) and *market* (n). Sometimes the pronunciation of the two forms is different, such as *to produce* (v) and *produce* (n). Other words that follow the same pattern are: *subject, object, transfer, prospect, record, progress, survey, refund*

🎧 1 B   Listen to the statements (A–H) and choose the one that best describes each picture.

C   Now listen again and identify the verbs. How many synonyms can you find for the verbs that are used?

Listening 1

A Look at the items below. What are the names for each of these things?

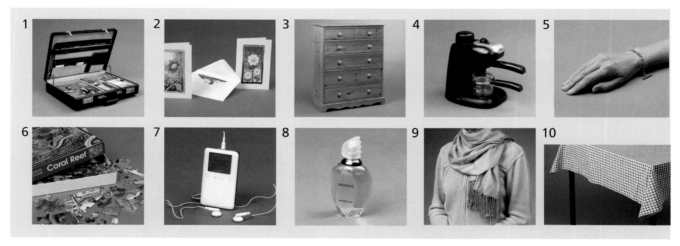

		FLOOR			FLOOR
STATIONERY		**2**	LEATHER GOODS		**0**
TV / HI-FI		**4**	ELECTRICAL APPLIANCES		**4**
HOME FURNISHINGS		**5**	HOUSEHOLD LINENS		**5**
TOYS AND GAMES		**3**	HAIR SALON		**2**
WOMEN'S FASHION		**1**	WELCOME AND INFO DESK		**0**
COSMETICS		**0**	CUSTOMER SERVICES		**2**
JEWELRY		**1**	TEENAGE FASHION		**3**

B Use the wall directory of the department store to locate where you would find items 1–10.

C Listen to three short conversations (1–3). Which department did these conversations take place in? What did the customer request in each conversation?

	Location	Request
1	*teenage fashion*	....
2	....	....
3	....	....

ACTIVE PRACTICE

Think about a product that you have bought recently and remember:

- your reasons for buying it
- where you bought it (department store, mail order, online, secondhand, etc.)
- the quality of the item
- the service
- the price

Meet with a partner and exchange information about your shopping experience.

Grammar Check 1

Comparatives and superlatives

When we talk about differences and similarities, we use the comparative.
*The new models are **smaller**, **less expensive** and a little **lighter than** the old ones but they're not **as powerful**.*
We use the superlative to talk about the qualities that make something unique.
*The Christmas period is **the busiest** and **the most profitable** time of the year for retailers.*

A Look at the examples and answer the questions.

1 How do you form comparatives and superlatives from:
   a   one- or two-syllable adjectives?
   b   two- or more syllable adjectives that end in *y*?
   c   three- or more syllable adjectives?
2 Which words are used with comparative adjectives to express:
   a   similarity?
   b   difference?
3 Is the article *the* used before:
   a   a comparative?
   b   a superlative?

see page 131 in the Grammar Reference section

B Some of the comparatives and superlatives in the slogans are incorrect. Identify the errors and correct them.

Advertising Slogans

1 **Our repairmen are the ~~lonelier~~ guys in town.**
   loneliest

2 *It's better than anything.*

3 **The more REFRESHING drink in the WORLD.**

4 If only everything in life was as reliable than a Volkswagen.

5 No battery is **strongest** for **longer**.

6 The world's more **trusted** anti-virus solution.

7 BEST A MAN CAN GET.

8 If you find it cheapest, we pay you the difference.

9 **ALWAYS the lowest price. ALWAYS.**

Viewpoint

Look at the pictures. What do they communicate about the values of the Camper company?

A Scan the four texts (A–D) below about the Spanish company Camper. In which of the texts would you expect to find information about the following things?

1 how the company was created
2 new store concepts
3 Camper's restaurant business
4 food preparation
5 unique footwear features
6 interior design

CAMPER

A HISTORY

Camper is the living story of a family business and of a family who have been working together for over a century – the story of four generations that have dedicated their life's work to the footwear industry. In 1877, Antonio Fluxa, a shoe craftsman, set sail for England to learn about the latest industrial manufacturing techniques. On his return, he introduced the first shoemaking machines. In 1975, Lorenzo Fluxa created Camper and in 1981, the first Camper store was opened in Barcelona. Today Camper has over 1,000 carefully selected points of sale in 20 countries.

B CAMPER FOODBALL

The eating place – built on the principles of bioconstruction, using non-contaminating materials and renewable energy sources – is an ecological space where you can eat alone or with company. Here people sit on steps designed for a full sensorial experience – a space for conversation and also for reverie.

Nothing to hide – we're offering simple, healthy and natural cuisine, free from any secrets. For this reason you can always watch us preparing the food. Camper Foodball is an eating space designed to share food culture.

CAMPER

B Now read through the texts a second time and answer the following questions.

1 Which cities have info-stores?
2 Where was the first Camper store opened?
3 How many stores in the world sell Camper shoes?
4 What seating arrangements do Foodball restaurants have?
5 How are Foodball restaurants different from traditional ones?
6 What can you find inside an info-shop?
7 What was the inspiration for the Mutante shoe?
8 What is the most unusual feature of the Mutante shoe?

C INFO-SHOP, MADRID

D MUTANTE

The design for this new line was inspired by the old boxing glove and the result ... a new concept with a unique aesthetic and a personality of its own. The Mutante is based on an advanced manufacturing process known as the "glove" concept, providing maximum comfort and protection for your feet.

Special padded leathers that are extremely soft and, at the same time, resistant, give this shoe a more "retro" look. The lining, made of a natural material known as Climatex, provides protection against impact and temperature control, while the insole, of natural materials like cocolatex and wool, cushions the foot when walking. But the most unique feature of this revolutionary shoe will be a surprise for more than a few of you! There is no left or right! Each shoe can be used for the left or right foot.

Camper's third info-shop has opened in the well-known Salamanca area of Madrid. The new store is in a prize location, at the corner of calle Serrano and calle Jorge Juan.

The store design is made up of images, icons and objects which are joined by Camper shoes to create an enormous visual Camper encyclopedia with more than 900 references. The store becomes a museum for the visitor to experience.

As in the other info-shops (London and Tokyo) the decoration becomes the information and the information becomes the decoration.

Listening 2

  Listen to a radio report about a new Camper business venture and complete the notes below.

New sector of activity: ....

Location: ....

Unique features: ....

Customer feedback: ....

Future plans: ....

Vocabulary Builder

Separable prefixes

Separable prefixes can be added to the base form of some words to give them a different meaning. Some common prefixes are:

dis	re	inter	un	~~over~~	under
mis	bi	co	sub	out	up

A Which of these prefixes can be added to give the following meanings?

1 to an excessive degree   ...*over*...load
2 once more, again   ....fill
3 two   ....lingual
4 between, among   ....active
5 less than, insufficiently   ....age
6 improved, high   ....grade
7 under, below   ....contract
8 together with   ....operate
9 not   ....sold
10 badly, incorrectly   ....manage
11 better or more than   ....do
12 removal, reversal   ....continue

s iPRESS

B Which prefix can be added to each of the following groups of words?

1	...*up*...	market	date	scale	swing	turn
2	....	stock	pay	charge	priced	size
3	....	direct	inform	judge	lead	represent
4	....	satisfied	like	regard	place	approve
5	....	act	fund	position	design	pay
6	....	standard	divide	group	total	section

C Complete the following sentences by adding an appropriate prefix to the words in italics.

1 Retailers are required to provide wheelchair access for ...*dis*...*abled* customers.
2 I just checked the receipt and realized that I've been ....*charged* by more than five dollars.
3 The store manager wants to ....*negotiate* the terms of the lease.
4 This particular model has been ....*continued*.
5 ....*management* of the inventory leads to lower levels of sales.
6 It is easy to ....*estimate* the impact that a successful advertising campaign can have.
7 We specialize in fashionable and affordable ....*size* clothing and footwear.

D Other common separable prefixes are: *down-, en-, ex-, extra-, hyper-, im-, in-, non-, super-*. Make a list of words that begin with these prefixes and then compare your list with a partner.

Grammar Check 2

Tag questions

> Tag questions are used to confirm information or to seek agreement. We make tag questions by adding an inverted auxiliary verb (or tag) at the end of a statement.
>
> *It's not possible to buy directly through the Internet,* **is it**?
> ⬇   ⬇
> statement   question
> ⬆   ⬆
> *These sunglasses are made in France,* **aren't they**?

● see page 132 in the Grammar Reference section

A Look at the examples above and complete the rules for tag questions.

When the statement is in the negative, the tag question is in the ....
When the statement is in the affirmative, the tag question is in the ....

B A customer is asking a sales clerk for more information about the Segway. Complete each question with the appropriate tag.

1 There's no problem using the Segway in shopping malls, *is there* ?   (.....)
2 The warranty covers all mechanical defects for one year, ...?   (.....)
3 The orientation sessions for new Segway drivers aren't obligatory, ...?   (.....)
4 I don't need to check tire pressure every day, ...?   (A)
5 It won't take more than an hour to assemble the machine, ...?   (.....)
6 Delivery will be made directly to my home, ...?   (.....)
7 You said that you had the accessories in stock, ...?   (.....)
8 You couldn't give me a discount on that price, ...?   (.....)

Listening 3

  Listen to the sales clerk's responses (A–H) and match them with the customer's questions about the Segway. Write your answers in the spaces provided in the previous exercise.

Communication

Presenting a product

You work in the marketing department of a mail-order company which sells selected consumer products through its monthly catalog *The Best Buyers' Guide*.

The new edition of the brochure is now almost complete. However, two products you had planned to include are no longer available. A meeting has been called to select two replacement products for the catalog.

Choose one of the role cards on page 170 and prepare a short presentation of a product.
Form a group with other students and take turns presenting. Decide which two products your group will include in the catalog.

5 Industry

Snapshot

A   Look at the pictures. What is being made, built, or manufactured? What equipment is being used? What work clothing are the people wearing?

1

2

3

4

 B   Listen to the statements (A–H) and choose two that describe each picture.

Grammar Check 1

The passive

The passive is often used to describe a process and to focus on the action.
The emphasis is on **what** is being done rather than **who** is doing it.

> The workers *are mixing* the raw materials in large basins.
> The raw materials *are being mixed* in large basins (by the workers).

A Look at the examples. Which sentence focuses on:

1 **what** is being done?
2 **who** is doing it?

B Now look at two sentences written in the passive and complete the grammar rule.

> The components *were assembled* in a factory overseas.
> The skyscraper *will be built* in less than eight months.

● see page 132 in the Grammar Reference section

The passive is formed by using the appropriate form of the auxiliary verb ....
+ the .... participle form of the main verb.

C Read the story of Jelly Belly's sweet success. Then go on a factory tour where you will learn how Jelly Belly jelly beans are manufactured. The production process is composed of eight steps.

Jelly Belly

The Original Gourmet

Jelly Bean

Jelly Belly's sweet beginnings are traced back to the Goelitz brothers Gustav and Albert, who emigrated from Germany to the United States and began making and selling sweets in 1869. Today, the fourth generation of the Goelitz family still carry on the tradition of making candy. The company is most famous for its gourmet jelly beans.

Jelly Belly Factory Tour

As you read steps 1 to 3 of the Factory Tour, <u>underline</u> the verbs in the passive.

Tour Floor plan

Warehouse

Robotic Palletizing

8 Packaging

Finishing **6**

7

Panning **5**

Coating **4**

Raw Materials

Auto Dryroom **3**

1 Kitchen Mogul **2**

Manual Dryroom **3**

Office

STEP 1 — Getting Centered

A Jelly Belly jelly bean starts with its center. First, sugars, flavors, and colors <u>are blended</u> in large kettles. Then many delicious ingredients are added to make the incredible flavors.

STEP 2 — Taking Shape

When the candy is cooked to perfection, small amounts of the hot liquid candy are dropped by a machine into individual depressions, creating 1,260 Jelly Belly centers on each tray.

STEP 3 — Firming Up

Now the trays are transferred to drying rooms to cool and firm up overnight.

D For steps 4 and 5, write the past participle of the verbs in parentheses.

STEP 4 — A Short Sugar Shower

The next day, the firm centers are [1](send) ......*sent*.... through a moisture steam bath and a sugar shower. Once they are [2](sugarcoat) .... the centers rest for 24 to 48 hours before being [3](give) .... their outer shells.

STEP 5 — The Most Engrossing Part

Two hundred pounds of Jelly Belly centers are [4](heap) .... into a rotating drum, which is [5](call) .... an "engrossing pan". Four layers of syrups and sugar are [6](add) .... by hand, building the flavored shells around the centers over a two-hour period.

E Complete the tour by filling in the passive form of the appropriate verb from the list.

STEP 6 — The Polishing Point

Four hundred pounds of Jelly Belly beans [7] ...*are poured*.... into revolving stainless-steel pans. Confectioner's glaze [8]................ over the tumbling beans. Each bean [9]................ to a high-gloss finish. Then the shiny jelly beans [10]................ on pallets for two to four days.

sift
polish
season
~~pour~~

STEP 7 — Name That Bean

Each Jelly Belly bean [11]................ into its own pocket on a tray of a printing machine. When the jelly beans pass under a very soft roller, the Jelly Belly name [12]................ on every bean.

print
insert

STEP 8 — Packed, Stacked, and Shipped

Once the Jelly Belly jelly beans [13]................,they [14]................ onto huge trucks and [15]................ to candy stores, supermarkets, and gourmet food stores.

transport
package
load

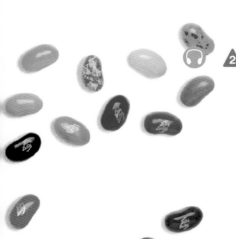

Listening 1

2 Read the five questions commonly asked by visitors at the end of the Jelly Belly tour. Then listen to the tour guide's responses (A–E) and match them with the questions.

1 How many tons of Jelly Belly jelly beans are made in a year? ....
2 How are new flavors for Jelly Belly beans created? ....
3 How many flavors are manufactured? ....
4 Are Jelly Belly beans marketed only in the United States? ....
5 Is it true that Jelly Belly jelly beans were the first jelly beans in outer space? ....

Vocabulary Builder

Synonyms and antonyms

> Synonyms are words or phrases with similar meanings.
> He **lost** the plans. = He **misplaced** the plans.
> Antonyms are words or phrases with opposite meanings.
> Instead of **reducing** production, the company has decided to **expand** its line.

A Place a check (✓) next to the synonyms and a cross (✗) next to the antonym in each word list (1–4).

1	2	3	4
mended ✓	maintained	modernized	stored
repaired ✓	neglected	outdated	gotten rid of
damaged ✗	serviced	renovated	thrown away
fixed	....	....	....

B Now add one of the following synonyms to each list.

looked after   discarded   refurbished   ~~fixed~~

5 C Complete the sentences with the correct form of a word or phrase from each list (1–4).

1 The foundry is outmoded and needs to be *modernized*.
2 Equipment that has been .... is dangerous. All machinery should be properly cared for.
3 Chemicals should not be kept beyond the expiration date, but must be ....
4 The holding tank is broken and needs to be ....

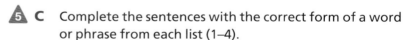

D Circle the word or phrase in sentences 1–4 that is an antonym of the word you used to complete the sentence.

Listening 2

Troubleshooting

Some TOEIC® questions involve "troubleshooting situations" where the speakers are discussing a problem and the action that should be taken.

  A Listen to the five conversations (A–E) and identify the industrial problems the speakers are discussing.

1 A tank is leaking. ....
2 Safety equipment has been removed. ....
3 There are no spare parts. ....
4 Operation costs are too high. ....
5 The raw materials have been contaminated. ....
6 Someone is not wearing protective gear. ....
7 Items have been damaged. ...A....

B Listen to the conversations again and select the solutions to the five problems.

1 Safety clothing is made available. ....
2 An order should be placed immediately. ....
3 The factory should be automated. ....
4 A report should be made. A
5 The missing equipment should be put back in place. ....
6 Hazardous waste should be safely discarded. ....
7 The processing plant should be shut down. ....

C While visiting an overseas factory as a site inspector, you find that many of the mandatory safety signs have errors. Identify the error and make the corrections.

1 HARD HATS MUST BE ~~WEARING~~ AT ALL TIMES.
..........worn..........

2 PREVENTIVE MAINTENANCE PROCEDURES MUST BE CONDUCT EVERY FIVE DAYS.
....

3 WORK-RELATED ACCIDENTS SHOULD BEEN REPORTED IMMEDIATELY.
....

4 ALL TEXTILE MILL WORKERS IS EXPECTED TO SHOW THEIR BADGES UPON ENTRY.
....

5 THE SHOP FLOOR MUST BE KEEPING CLEAR AT ALL TIMES.
....

6 PLANT INSPECTION REPORTS MUST BE SIGNED FROM THE SUPERINTENDENT.
....

7 VISITORS TO THE REFINERY ARE ASK TO STAY BEHIND THE YELLOW LINES.
....

Viewpoint

What machines help you with everyday tasks?

 Read the article and letter. Then choose the best answer to the questions.

Robots to the rescue

By David Pilling

Of the world's 800,000 industrial robots busily welding and painting cars, 43.5% are operating in Japan, compared to 1.8% in Britain and 14% in the US.

Today, 70% of these machines are designed and built in Japan, which is also far ahead in developing human robots. Last month, a hospital in Fukushima took delivery of three robots – a blue receptionist and two green

helpers to guide people to elevators and carry their bags.

Yoichi Takamoto of Tmsuk, the company that manufactured the devices, says, "Right from the start we decided to make robots that are not toys, but rather robots that are able to do something humans cannot do."

Tmsuk is working on rescue robots able to withstand intense heat and to work in collapsed buildings. Its emergency robot, developed with the fire department, has a 12-meter arm span and giant hands able to lift a car.

Banryu, a security-guard robot fitted with infra-red sensors, smoke detectors, and cameras, is a good example of how household robots might develop from futuristic fantasy to viable tools. Even if halfway around the world, users can operate it by cell phone, getting it to send pictures to a 3G handset. If it senses an intruder, Banryu calls the

owner, relaying pictures of the suspicious incident.

"Automation of menial tasks, or ones too difficult or dangerous for humans, will help solve multiple economic problems, including how to compete with foreign labor and replenish the domestic workforce," says Shin Takayama. In a recent book, he argues that robot technology will become one of Japan's main competitive advantages: "Robots will come to Japan's rescue."

Dear Mr. Takamoto,

My company, BizzTrak, is a business advisory service specializing in providing research and business intelligence for our many corporate customers around the world. We have recently received an inquiry from an executive director of an international hotel group, requesting background and technical information about small-sized service robots. We would be very interested in obtaining more detailed information about one of the robots that you manufacture, Roborior. Concerning its voice recognition capability, does Roborior understand and speak other languages than Japanese? As your website is mostly in Japanese, could you make the Roborior product information available to us in English and also provide a price list?

Best regards,
Jay O'Leary

⚠ TOEIC® Tip

Part 7 includes four Double Passages, which each present two different, but related documents (a letter and an email, an ad and a letter, etc.). Make sure you give yourself enough time for the Double Passages. Look for the links between the two documents. You may even want to start Part 7 by doing the Double Passages first.

1 Which of the following robot-assisted tasks is NOT mentioned?
   A Welding and painting automobiles.
   B Guiding people and carrying luggage.
   C Guarding and conducting surveillance.
   D Manufacturing smoke detectors and cameras.

2 Who does Jay O'Leary work for?
   A A robot manufacturer.
   B A business consultancy.
   C A hotel chain.
   D A hospital.

DISCUSSION

What tasks would you like to see automated?
How would you feel about living and working with robots?

Grammar Check 2

Causative verbs

> We use causative verbs to indicate that a person causes or enables another person to do something.
>
> **Type1**
>
> The director — had   the technicians install robots on the production line.
> made   the plant manager work overtime.
> let   the factory workers go home early.
>
> **Type 2**
>
> The director — got   them to install robots on the production line.
> forced   him to work overtime.
> allowed them to go home early.
>
> **Type 3**
>
> The director — had / got   robots installed on the production line (by the technicians).

A Look at the examples in the box and answer the following questions to complete the grammar rules.

1 Which causative verbs are followed by:
   - the direct object + an infinitive with *to*? ....
   - the direct object + an infinitive without *to*? ....
   - the direct object + a past participle? ....

see page 132 in the Grammar Reference section

2 Which type 2 verbs are synonymous with *have*, *make*, and *let* in type1?
3 Can you think of other verbs that can be used as causatives?

5 B Choose the word or phrase that best completes the sentence.

1 The foreman is making the crew (re-install ✓ / to re-install) the light fixtures.
2 We must get the site plans (approve / approved) before we begin construction.
3 The plant supervisor is having outside experts (inspect / to inspect) the damage.
4 We need to have the assembly line repaired (from / by) the mechanic.
5 The supervisor let the mill workers (take / to take) an extra eight-minute break.
6 The union representatives convinced management (increase / to increase) safety measures.
7 They'll (have / make) the report printed and bundled by the publications office.
8 The technician programmed the robot (transfer / to transfer) the croissants.

Listening 3

Save or scrap: building upon the past

🎧 ④ Listen carefully to the news report and complete the archeologist's notes.

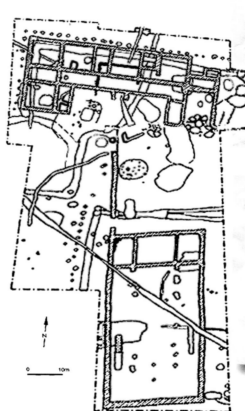

DATE: January 15

LOCATION: Construction site at 14th and Salem
near the waterfront.
Site designation: [1] *an industrial park*.
is being built.
Site or objects discovered: Large
settlement, extensive ruins, many
items including [2]...........................
Ruins discovered by [3]...................... .

SITE CONDITIONS:
Excellent. Very little damage – a
major discovery.

Next public meeting on Tuesday
January 22 at the [4]...........................

COMMUNICATION

Construction and development versus preservation and heritage

You are going to take part in the planning commission meeting to discuss the future of the Metropolitan industrial park. Should the ancient settlement be documented but then covered by the industrial park? Or should the plans for the industrial park be abandoned so that the ancient settlement can be preserved and a museum and cultural center be built? What is worth more to the city – business development or cultural heritage?

Decide which role you would like to play in the meeting and then read your role card on page 170.

⚠ TOEIC® Tip

In Part 4 of the test, pay special attention to the start of the talk. Identify the speaker and the purpose of the talk. Listen for the main ideas.

6 Trade

Snapshot

A Look at the pictures and describe what the people are doing.

1

2

3

4

B Now match the vocabulary with the pictures.

financial market	cargo containers	international port
auction house	artwork	wholesale food market
fruit and produce	stocks and commodities	

C Choose two pictures and write one statement for each.

  D Listen to the statements (A–H) and choose two that describe each picture.

Listening 1

The international art market

Art is one of the many commodities that circulate around the world. According to a European Fine Art Foundation survey, global art market sales annually exceed €26.7 billion.

  A The international art trade involves many of the import / export activities below. Listen to the five conversations (1–5) and identify which activity the speakers refer to.

bidding and purchasing	....
invoicing	....
packing	....
insuring	....
shipping	1
clearing customs and paying duties and tariffs	....
delivering and receiving	....

B Listen again and identify the keywords that give clues about the context.

Grammar Check 1

Future forms

Future time can be expressed in several different ways. Look carefully at the verb forms and time expressions in the examples below.

> 1 We're meeting with our shipping broker in three days.
> 2 Tomorrow's auction begins at 9:00 a.m.
> 3 The new trade agreement benefiting growers will go into effect by January.
> 4 She's going to place the order as soon as the price drops.

A Match the example sentences above with the list of different uses and then write in the verb forms to complete the grammar rules.

For future actions and predictions:	...........3, will + verb...........
For future plans or intentions:	....
For future arrangements that have already been made:	....
For schedules and timetables:	....

● see page 133 in the Grammar Reference section

⚠ TOEIC® Tip

Note which verb tense is used after *as soon as* in sentence 3 of exercise B. In phrases beginning with *as soon as, the moment, when*, the future is expressed in the present simple. *He'll invoice the importer when the shipment arrives.* (NOT ... *when it* ~~will arrive~~ *arrives*.)

5 B Choose the word or phrase that correctly completes the sentence.

1 A foreign agency will (*handle / handles / handling*) the crates.
2 If the agreement goes into effect, it (*will make / makes / is making*) it easier for all member countries to trade financial services.
3 He will fax the transit documents as soon as they (*are / will be / are going to be*) issued.
4 The moment the auction (*begin / begins / is beginning*), the bidding will be very competitive.
5 Who (*goes / is going / will have gone*) to Hong Kong for the meeting next week?
6 Our suppliers are opening a new showroom as soon as they (*receive / will receive / are receiving*) their importers' license.
7 Our warehouse manager (*will / go / is going*) to meet the transporter at the receiving dock.
8 The freight forwarder will notify the distributor when the consignment (*arrive / arrives / will arrive*).

Listening 2

 4 Listen to the report about the cost of a specialty coffee and complete the missing information.

Retail price of a
latte coffee: ¹ ....

Amounts	=	Costs
$1.35		² ....
³		rent, marketing, administration
$0.25		⁴ ....
⁵		cup and milk
$0.035		⁶ ....

Viewpoint

7 **A** Read the article to find out what can be done to help coffee growers.

Juan Valdez brews up a plan
Colombian coffee growers hope retail shops will keep them in beans.

Café de Colombia

The Colombian Coffee Federation, which represents more than 500,000 Colombian coffee growers, is planning to enter the U.S. specialty coffee market by early next year with the opening of its first Juan Valdez coffee shops.

Gabriel Silva, the president of the federation, said he believes the coffee growers have been "too passive" in claiming a larger piece of the U.S. $8.4 billion specialty coffee industry.

"In a cup of coffee that you get at a coffee shop, between one and two cents goes back to the farmer," Silva said. "We need to build our own solutions and really fight for our share of the industry." Coffee growers are facing a difficult market. Per-capita consumption has been in decline since 1963, with the only growth area being the specialty coffee shops, according to the International Coffee Organization in London.

Because of a global surplus from countries like Vietnam and Brazil, the price of coffee beans has also declined significantly. In Colombia today, the average coffee grower gets "only about U.S.$0.68 per pound of coffee," Silva said.

Industry trade groups have tried to reduce coffee farmers' losses by encouraging them to destroy oversupply and raise prices. They have also urged food companies to buy fairtrade coffee, which guarantees a so-called living wage to poor coffee producers in developing countries.

By selling their own coffee at their own coffee shops, the federation plans to return between U.S.$0.04 and U.S.$0.05 for each cup of coffee sold. "Each of the federation's farmers will also have an ownership stake in the shops," Silva said.

The profits from the retail operation will go back to the federation, which said it would put marketing dollars into the Juan Valdez brand and work to improve Colombia's coffee-growing regions by building access roads, schools, health centers, and housing. "It's certainly interesting," John Glass, a restaurant analyst at CIBC World Markets said of the plan.

B Complete the notes with information from the text.

1 the planned opening date for stores ....
2 the revenue of the U.S. specialty market ....
3 the only industry growth sector ....
4 the revenue Colombian farmers will receive (per cup) ....
5 four projects to be financed by Juan Valdez profits ....

DISCUSSION

What do you think of the Colombian Coffee Federation's plan?
What other solutions exist?

Grammar Check 2

Cause and effect

We use the following verbs to express cause and effect relationships.

to result in / from*	to originate (from)
to cause	to be responsible (for)
to lead to	to mean

*Prepositions can modify the relationship between cause and effect.

The poor harvest resulted *from* inadequate rainfall.
Inadequate rainfall resulted *in* a poor harvest.

● see page 133 in the Grammar Reference section

We can also use nouns and linking expressions to express cause and effect.

Nouns	*Linking expressions*
the cause (of) the reason (for)	because (of) since as due to
the effect (of) the result (of) the outcome	so as a result therefore consequently thus

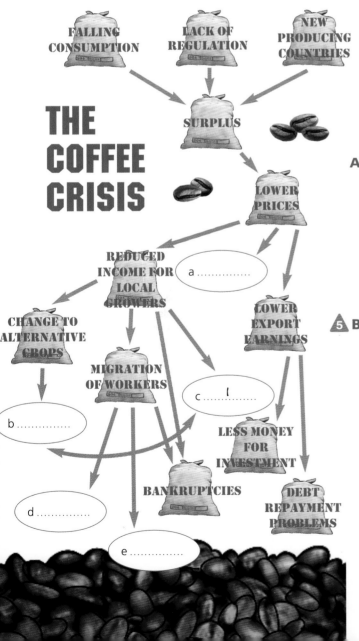

A **In which of the blanks in the chart would you include the following effects?**

1 Standards of living fall.
2 Women have to take on a heavier workload.
3 Multinational coffee companies can increase their profits.
4 Men move to find better paid work.
5 Illicit crops are introduced.

5 B **Complete the sentences based on the information in the chart. Use the appropriate words to express cause and effect.**

1 There are three main ...*reasons*... for the current crisis.
2 The combination of these three factors has .... a situation where too much coffee is being produced.
3 As a direct .... of this, the price of raw coffee beans has dropped by 30%.
4 The multiple .... of this decrease have transformed local economies and deprived governments of export earnings.
5 .... countries receive less money from exports, they are forced to cut back on public services.

Listening 3

Meetings

Trade agreements are often reached in meetings. The trading partners come together in order to exchange ideas before exchanging goods and services.

2 A **What words are missing from these questions frequently heard in meetings? Listen and fill in the blanks.**

1 Could someone take the ....*minutes*...., please?   .....B.....
2 Has everyone received a copy of the ....?   ....
3 Could we move on to the next ....?   ....
4 What are your .... on this issue?   ....
5 Why don't we take a ten-minute ....?   ....
6 Is there any other ....?   ....
7 Who would like to .... the next meeting?   ....

B **Now write the words next to their definitions.**

1 lead ....
2 subject to be discussed or action to be taken ....
3 pause ....
4 the meeting schedule ....
5 topic ....
6 opinions ....
7 notes or record of what is said ...*minutes*....

What other meanings do these words have in different contexts?

2 C **Now listen to seven questions, each followed by two responses, and choose the correct response. Write your answers (a or b) in the spaces provided in exercise A.**

⚠ TOEIC® Tip

Incorrect responses in Part 2 of the test incorporate words that are "distracters." These words often have more than one meaning.
In exercise C question 1, we hear the word *minutes*. This could mean a written record of what is discussed in a meeting or a reference to time, 60 minutes = one hour.
Pay careful attention to the context in order to determine the correct meaning of the word.

Vocabulary Builder

Idiomatic expressions 1: *point*

A You can strengthen your active vocabulary by building on words
you already know.
How many expressions can you think of that use the word *point*?
Match each of the expressions (1–6) with its definition (a–f).

1 to make a point
2 to point out
3 point of view
4 to the point
5 beside the point
6 pointless

a an attitude or opinion
b relevant and appropriate
c with no aim or purpose
d irrelevant
e to explain fully one's idea
f to draw attention to

5 B Fill in the blanks with the most appropriate expression.

1 That's ..*beside the point*.. It doesn't have anything to do with the main issue.
2 A good broker should .... all the important clauses in a shipping contract.
3 I see what you mean, but I'm not sure I agree with your ....
4 We don't need to rush order this shipment. It's ....; the carrier won't be
leaving the docks until next week.
5 The chairperson's comments were .... She's always precise.
6 When Sanjay ...., he is always very persuasive.

C Building on words you already know will help you score points on the TOEIC®.
Find other idiomatic expressions with the words: *head, back, face*, and *hand*.

MANKOFF

"Good point, Remson. You couldn't be more right if you were me."

Communication

Fair trade or free trade?

A Read the extract from a Fairtrade brochure and answer the questions.

1 What are the objectives of the Fairtrade Foundation?
2 How can towns participate in Fairtrade programs?

Five Goals for a Fairtrade Town, City or Zone

The purpose of a Fairtrade Town is to contribute to the Fairtrade Foundation's aim of tackling poverty. Supporting the FAIRTRADE Mark helps disadvantaged producers from poorer countries to receive a better deal. To become a Fairtrade Town, five goals must be met:

1 The local council must pass a resolution* supporting Fairtrade, and serve Fairtrade coffee and tea at its meetings and in offices and canteens.

2 A range of Fairtrade products must be readily available in the area's shops and served in local cafés and catering establishments (targets are set in relation to population).

3 Fairtrade products must be used by a number of local work places (real-estate agencies, hairdressers, etc.) and community organizations (churches, schools, etc.).

4 The council must attract popular support for the campaign.

5 A local Fairtrade steering group* must be convened to ensure continued commitment to Fairtrade Town status.

FAIRTRADE ®

Guarantees **a better deal** for Third World Producers

A selection of the Fairtrade range

A meeting will be held at
7 p.m. on Saturday November 26th
at the town hall to discuss the following question:

IS FAIRTRADE STATUS IN THE INTERESTS OF OUR COMMUNITY?

Meeting Agenda

1 Presentations
2 Discussion of the Fairtrade application
3 Vote on whether or not to apply for Fairtrade Town status

Glossary

*to pass a resolution — to adopt an official decision after a group or organization have voted

*steering group — a group of people who are chosen to direct the way something is dealt with

B Your town council has set up a meeting to decide whether to apply for Fairtrade status. Choose one of the role cards on pages 170–171 and prepare a short presentation of your reasons for supporting or opposing the town's Fairtrade application.

Units 4–6

🎧 Listening Test

Part 1

Directions: Listen to the four recorded statements for each picture. Choose the statement that best describes what you see in the picture.

3

1

4

2

Part 2

Directions: You will hear nine recorded questions each followed by three responses. Choose the best response for each question.

5	A	B	C
6	A	B	C
7	A	B	C
8	A	B	C
9	A	B	C
10	A	B	C
11	A	B	C
12	A	B	C
13	A	B	C

Part 3

Directions: Listen to the two conversations and answer the three questions that are asked about each conversation.

14 Where does this conversation take place?
A   In an interview
B   In a meeting
C   At an auction
D   At customs

15 What does the man say they need to do?
A   Create a new committee
B   Replace some furniture
C   Cancel an appointment
D   Choose a new chairperson

16 When will the nominations probably be discussed?
A   Next week
B   In two weeks
C   Next month
D   Next year

17 What's the problem?
A   The man does not like the fabrics.
B   The material will have to be copied
C   The factory was not insured
D   The shipment arrived damaged

18 Where does the woman most likely work?
A   A shipping company
B   An insurance company
C   A fashion store
D   A recording studio

19 What does the man want to know?
A   When payment will be made
B   Where to send the documents
C   Who to contact
D   How much money he will receive

Part 4

Directions: Listen to the two short talks and answer three questions on each.

20 Who is the speaker?
A   The facilities manager
B   A researcher
C   A lab technician
D   A construction worker

21 When will construction be complete?
A   In a year
B   In six months
C   By Monday
D   As of next week

22 What must authorized personnel do in order to enter the site?
A   Inform their colleagues
B   Put on special clothes
C   Read the safety memo
D   Sign a release form

23 Which of the following is NOT a reason for the crisis in the industry?
A   Low prices
B   Quotas
C   Overproduction
D   Falling demand

24 What was the role of the International Coffee Federation?
A   To finance farmers
B   To promote new farming methods
C   To limit coffee production
D   To market coffee products

25 According to the news report, what have mechanized production techniques led to?
A   Higher prices
B   Larger quantities
C   Better quality
D   More regulation

Reading Test

Part 5

Directions: Choose the one word or phrase that best completes the sentence.

26 The crates were .... by freight train.
   A   transport
   B   transports
   C   transported
   D   be transported

27 Food retailers who do not .... to the new regulations on food storage and handling will be liable to fines.
   A   inform
   B   perform
   C   conform
   D   reform

28 An international team is going .... the new facilities.
   A   visit
   B   to visit
   C   visiting
   D   visitors

29 We should make .... of meeting more regularly.
   A   an appointment
   B   an agenda
   C   an item
   D   a point

30 We'll begin reviewing the proposals as soon as the bidding period ....
   A   be closed
   B   will close
   C   closes
   D   close

31 The study shows that retired people often .... shopping as more of a leisure activity.
   A   preview
   B   interview
   C   review
   D   view

32 Customers who return goods within 14 days will be entitled to a full .... on the purchase price.
   A   refund
   B   renewal
   C   replacement
   D   restoration

33 Consumer protection laws prohibit advertisers from making .... claims.
   A   unfulfilled
   B   insufficient
   C   misleading
   D   distrustful

34 Earnings from exports have fallen sharply .... fluctuations on the international currency markets.
   A   since
   B   due to
   C   consequently
   D   because

35 Any further reduction in prices will inevitably .... that suppliers will see their profits reduced.
   A   lead
   B   result
   C   mean
   D   cause

36 We've asked three freight companies to give us quotes for the job and we'll take whichever one is the ....
   A   cheaper
   B   cheapest
   C   cheaply
   D   cheap

37 If we are unable to supply any item that you have ordered, you .... by email.
   A   will be notified
   B   will notify
   C   are notifying
   D   notify

Part 6

Directions: Four words or phrases are missing in the text. Choose the best answer to complete each empty space in the text.

Questions 38–41 refer to the following email.

To: Regional Store Managers
From: Anna Stanton, Quality Control Manager
Subject: Recall of Blue Canyon cheese

My department has been alerted ....
38 A with
       B by
       C from
       D to
the food and health authority. They have identified production irregularities in some batches of Blue Canyon cheese. Although this does not represent a severe health hazard, Blue Canyon has decided to recall all products from distribution centers and retail outlets across the country.

Initial reports suggest that the ....
39 A cause
       B effect
       C reason
       D outcome
of the problem may have been the use of improperly treated water at the production plant. Production of Blue Canyon products will not resume until the health inspection authorities ....
40 A is going to complete
       B is completing
       C will complete
       D complete
their investigation.

Please ....
41 A ask
       B have
       C let
       D make
your staff to remove all Blue Canyon products immediately and to post copies of the enclosed warning notice where the products were displayed in your store.

If you have any questions, please call my office directly.

Yours sincerely,
Anna Stanton
Quality Control Manager

Part 7

Directions: Read the following texts and choose the one best answer to each question.

Questions 42–44 refer to the following notice.

When you transport your goods internationally, several precautions must be taken to ensure proper shipment. Export shipments require greater handling than domestic transport and should be properly packaged and correctly documented so that they arrive safely and on time. You also need to make sure that breakable items are protected, and that other fragile goods will not be damaged by the stresses of air and ocean shipment, such as vibration and moisture.

You must first decide what mode of transport is best. When shipping within a continent, you may prefer land transportation. When shipping to another continent, the preferred method may be by sea or air. Although maritime shipping is generally less expensive than air, it can be much slower and thus less cost-effective. You should consider the additional costs of sea freight, such as surface transportation to and from the docks and port charges. Ocean freight can take longer than air freight and you may have to wait until the ship reaches its destination to receive payment.

42 What is the purpose of this notice?
A To inform freight forwarders about weight limitations
B To advise importers about insurance policies
C To provide general information about shipping
D To notify exporters about new safety measures

43 According to the document, shipping by sea usually:
A is best
B costs more
C is faster
D costs less

44 What additional cost can arise when using maritime freight?
A More expensive packaging
B Land transportation to and from the port
C More documentation
D Higher insurance premiums

Questions 45–47 refer to the following newspaper article.

European retailers are busy preparing the supermarkets of the future for shoppers from the past. The average age of European shoppers has already started its spectacular rise: from 38 today to 52 by 2050. This demographic shift is the direct result of the combination of increased longevity and lower birthrates. In some European Union countries, as much as one third of the population will be over 50 by the year 2015. So how will supermarkets cater to their ageing clientele? In Vienna, the German company Adeg Aktiv thinks it may have found the answer. Their new superstores, like the one the company is currently piloting, will feature some intriguing innovations; products will be labeled in larger print, shelves will be lower to provide easy access and shopping carts will have fold down seats to give tired shoppers an instant break.

The employees will also be selected from an older age group, the over-fifties. That fits nicely with the store's new 50+ trademark. Just how successful the new concept will be remains to be seen but there are some very positive signs; more than half of the customers in the pilot store are actually under the age of fifty. They were simply attracted by the shopper-friendly design of the stores and by the high standard of customer service.

45 Why is Adeg introducing a new supermarket concept?
A To target older shoppers
B To compete with rival stores
C To lower recruitment costs
D To attract a younger clientele

46 How old are the majority of customers in the pilot store?
A Between fifty and sixty years old
B At least fifty years old
C Less than fifty years old
D Under thirty years old

47 Which of the following is NOT a feature of the new stores?
A Specially designed shopping carts
B Personal shopping assistants
C Easy to read labels
D Easy to reach products

Questions 48–50 refer to the following notice.

Safety Notice

All employees should familiarize themselves with the following revisions to our "Safe Workplace" guidelines.

Footwear

As part of our policy to reduce the risk of injury and to promote safe work practices, WoodTech has revised its guidelines on appropriate footwear for the workplace.

- All employees working in designated "risk zones" (production, warehousing, and loading facilities) must wear protective shoes at all times. Protective footwear refers to shoes that have reinforced steel toecaps and that conform to the specifications of the National Work Safety Code (NWSC 202).
- Employees who do not work in designated "risk zones" or whose work does not require the lifting of heavy objects are required to wear appropriate safe footwear. Safe footwear includes only shoes that have low heels, non-slip soles, and leather uppers. Sandals, trainers, and slip-on shoes do not qualify as safe footwear.

All employees are reminded that they may be exposed to the risk of serious foot injury.

48 To whom does this notice apply?
- A   To WoodTech suppliers
- B   Only to sales personnel and trainers
- C   To clients visiting WoodTech facilities
- D   To everyone who works at WoodTech

49 According to the notice, why must someone wear appropriate footwear?
- A   To increase production
- B   To qualify for a promotion
- C   To decrease the risk of accidents
- D   To give a good impression to clients

50 When do employees have to put on protective shoes?
- A   When working anywhere in the company
- B   When the floors are wet and slippery
- C   When working outside "risk zones"
- D   When working within "risk zones"

7 Leisure

Snapshot

A   Look at the pictures. Where are the people? What are they doing?

1

2

3

4

⚠ TOEIC® Tip

In Part 1 of the test, the incorrect statements often contain distracting words that sound similar to or the same as words in the correct statement: (*ear/hear*) or (*here/hear*).
Make sure you listen to all of the statements before choosing the best answer.
Listen again to exercise B. What similar-sounding words are there to distract you?

🎧 ⚠ **B**   Listen to the statements (A–H) and choose the one that best describes each picture.

Listening 1

A   Match the country with its traditional recreational activity.

National Pastimes Quiz

1	Japan	a	pétanque
2	Russia	b	hurling
3	Ireland	c	mahjong
4	Malaysia	d	mushroom hunting
5	Finland	e	origami
6	U.K.	f	cricket
7	France	g	top-spinning
8	China	h	sauna

sauna cricket pétanque
origami
top-spinning
hurling

 B   Listen to the radio program discussing leisure trends in the United States and fill in the table.

National Leisure Trends

Top four leisure activities in the U.S.	Other activities	% who watch television	Top five recreational activities for 6	Top five recreational activities for 8 ....
1 .... reading socializing 2	using computers 3 .... watching spectator sports reading the newspaper	4 .... % once a day 57% < two hours 5 .... % > five hours	walking aerobics exercising 7 .... jogging	9 .... basketball walking 10 .... biking

DISCUSSION

What are the most popular forms of leisure and recreation in your country?
How do leisure trends in your country differ from those in the U.S.?
How do leisure and recreational activities differ between men and women?

Grammar Check 1

Relative pronouns: *that, who, whose, which, where*

Relative pronouns are used to combine two sentences.
My best friend loves to knit sweaters. My best friend lives in Norway.
*My best friend, **who** lives in Norway, loves to knit sweaters.*

A Look at the examples and answer the questions. Which relative pronoun(s):

● see page 133 in the Grammar Reference section

- is used only for people?
- can be used for things and people?
- is used for possessions?
- is used for places?

The neighbor *that* recommended this book is an avid reader.
My youngest brother, *who* works as a software engineer, enjoys playing computer games in his spare time.
Ivan, *whose* favorite pastime is dancing the tango, has been to Argentina several times.
Hobbies *that* require a lot of special equipment are expensive.
Origami, *which* is the ancient Japanese art of paper-folding, is now a world-wide pastime.
The ice-skating rink *where* I learned to play hockey is the home of the national champions.

B Combine the two sentences using a relative pronoun.

Svetlana taught me how to play chess. She won the national junior tournament.
1 ....

The Olympic Games are held every four years. They originated in Greece.
2 ....

My best friend can do the most amazing card tricks. His hobby is doing magic.
3 ....

C Choose the correct relative pronoun to complete the sentence.

1 One leisure activity (*that / who / whose*) has gained a large following in urban areas is rollerblading.
2 Steve Johnson, (*which / where / who*) grew up in Montana, loves to go trekking in the Himalayas.
3 Dragon-boat racing, (*who / which / whose*) is a popular sport in China, requires a lot of teamwork.
4 A major destination for surfers is Hawaii, (*where / which / who*) the waves can reach over 40 feet.
5 George, (*which / who / whose*) hobby is woodworking, has been my dance teacher for years.

Viewpoint

7 **A** Work in pairs. Each pair should read either the two Ⓐ texts or the two Ⓑ texts and answer the questions below:

1   What are the texts about?
2   Who are the people involved?
3   Where does the leisure activity take place?
4   How are the two texts related?

B Prepare two more questions about your texts. Exchange your questions with another pair who has been reading a different set of texts. Each pair should now read the second set of texts and answer the complete list of questions. Meet with the other pair and check your answers.

Ⓐ

Norway's COOLEST movie theater

BY LARS BEVANGER

The movie theater in the Norwegian town of Kautokeino is somewhat out of the ordinary. Not only is it entirely made out of snow – it is a drive-in. For snowmobiles.

Kautokeino is mainly populated with Samis, who are Norway's indigenous people, many of them reindeer farmers.

While they traditionally herded their reindeer using cross-country skis, the snowmobile is now an indispensable mode of transport for them.

"We wanted to give audiences the chance to drive down from the mountains into an outdoor movie theater," says Ms. Utsi, the leader of Kautokeino Sami film festival.

Snowmobile riders are shown documentaries, short films, and feature-length movies.

Anyone who wants to enjoy two hours under the stars in the high Arctic north of Norway needs to dress warmly. Temperatures here rarely rise above freezing.

In the words of audience member Per Ivar Jensen, "This is fantastic. You have a full moon, the very special Arctic light, and you can hardly see where the cinema ends and the Arctic wilderness begins."

Ⓐ

Delete   Reply   Reply All   Forward   Compose   Mailboxes   Get Mail   Junk   »

Hi Nukka,

I think you should submit your documentary film to the Sami Film Festival. It's a great opportunity to promote films such as yours that feature indigenous cultures. The festival website has an online submission form: http://www.samifilmfestival.com. You'll need to include: title of film, director, producer, running time, country, language, year of production, and a short synopsis. The deadline is March 1st.

Good luck and warmest wishes,

Lindsay

B

Far Off Course, Golf Becomes Adventure Sport

BY OTTO POHL

from *Golf Digest*

Cross-golf, which takes its name partially from cross-country, is also known as urban golf, X-golf, and turbo golf. In this version of golf, players choose the most unusual setting in which to try to get the ball into an improvised, predetermined hole. It can be played everywhere – through cities, from rooftops, and across vacant lots.

The game originated in Germany, Austria, and Switzerland and has become popular in Asia. The roots of European cross-golf go back to Hamburg ten years ago, when Torsten Schilling, traveling as a television producer, played golf in hotel corridors at night. Schilling founded the cross-golf group known as Natural Born Golfers and has now quit his day job to run it.

During their last tournament, Torsten Schilling and his team built a mock living room complete with couch, lamp, television, and table. After setting it adrift on a river, they stood on a boat and took turns trying to hit a golf ball through the television.

In cross-golf there are no rules, other than to have fun. Around the world, thousands are heading out into the urban wild, carrying golf clubs but otherwise free of any sense of golfing tradition.

For cross-golfers, freedom means not having to pay green fees.

B

Dear Mr. Singh,

Thank you for your letter offering us the opportunity to sponsor the cross-golf tournament that you are organizing in Jaipur, India. As a manufacturer of traditional golfing equipment, our company currently sponsors both well-known professional golfers and several major classic tournaments. While we support all efforts to promote the sport of golf to a wider public, we hope you will understand that sponsoring a cross-golf competition is not compatible with our role in the golfing community.

Sincerely,

Stanley Baker Johnston III

Premier Swing Limited
Producing the Finest in Golfing Equipment since 1877

DISCUSSION

How do leisure and recreational activities vary from place to place? From season to season? And from culture to culture?

MINH LONG

WORLD-FAMOUS ROAST CRAB
SINCE 1985

32 Main Street
San Diego, California

Closed Sundays • Banquet
Facilities Available

● *see page 134 in the Grammar Reference section*

Grammar Check 2

Indirect questions

We can make questions more polite by introducing them indirectly with polite question forms.

> What kind of restaurant *is it*?
> Can you tell me what kind of restaurant *it is*?

A Look at the questions above. What happens to the word order of the original question?

B Make the questions indirect by filling in the blanks.

1 Where can we find a good restaurant?
Would you happen to know where ....*we can find*........ a good restaurant?

2 Could you make a reservation for two, please?
I was wondering if .... a reservation for two, please?

3 How is the fish prepared?
Could you tell us how .... prepared?

4 What is today's dessert special?
I wonder what ....

mon Vieil ami

"A culinary experience"

Traditional and creative French cuisine

r e s t a u r a n t
331 Broad Street
New York, New York

Private Dining Room for Special Occasions

C Now listen to the questions and check your answers. What other questions would you hear in a restaurant?

Listening 2

 2 Listen to three questions (1–3) each followed by three responses (A–C). Choose the best response to each question.

1 .... 2 .... 3 ....

Skips SALMON HOUSE

SEATTLE'S FINEST SEAFOOD RESTAURANT

205 Southlake Drive
Seattle, Washington

ACTIVE PRACTICE

Imagine that you are planning a farewell dinner party for a friend or colleague. Prepare a list of questions to ask the restaurant manager who is helping you organize the event. Make some of your questions indirect by beginning them with one of the phrases below. With a partner take turns role-playing a planning meeting with a restaurant manager.

I wonder ...
Would you happen to know ...
Can you tell me ...

Do you know how / where / when / what ...
I was wondering if you could tell me ...

Vocabulary Builder

Participles used as adjectives: -ed versus -ing

> Participles are verb forms that can be used as adjectives.
> Look at the two statements.
> *The rules of some sports are very **confusing**.*
> *The visiting delegates were **confused** about the rules of baseball.*
> Present participles end in *-ing* and describe the effect a person or thing has on us.
> Past participles often end in *-ed* and are used to express how we feel about something.

A Read the first paragraph and identify the participle adjectives by <u>underlining</u> the present participles and (circling) the past participles.

If you're (tired) of the same old <u>boring</u> games, you might be interested in a new and exciting invention from the Interactive Institute in Sweden called BrainBall™. BrainBall is a game unlike others. What is most surprising about BrainBall is that the "winner" is the player who can stay relaxed under stress rather than the player who is aggressive and overly interested in winning. In order to win you have to be relaxed and not excited.

BrainBall™ by Moberg Research, Inc.

6 B Now complete the article with the correct form of the participle.

The players' brain waves are recorded and then processed to extract the alpha activity, which reflects a peaceful state of mind. The motion of a ball on the table is controlled by the difference in the alpha activity between the two players. If you are more ¹(*relax*) *relaxed* that is, more alpha, than your opponent, the ball rolls away from you toward your goal. Your opponent,

knowing he or she is losing, must relax further under this stress to reverse the direction of the ball. According to one enthusiastic player, "I was ²(*surprise*) .... to discover a game that I like! I get ³(*bore*) .... very quickly and find most board games ⁴(*tire*) .... But what makes BrainBall so ⁵(*interest*) .... and ⁶(*excite*) .... is that it's so ⁷(*relax*) ...."

ACTIVE PRACTICE

With a partner brainstorm a list of games and leisure activities. Interview another pair and find out how they feel about the activities on your list.

Are you interested in video games?
Actually, I prefer listening to music. It's so much more relaxing.
Don't you find Sudoku puzzles rather boring?
No. I really like them, especially if they're challenging.

Listening 3

A Look at the list of leisure activities below and brainstorm a list of words associated with each one.

.....1.... playing ping-pong or table tennis *tables with nets, paddles, balls*
.... swimming
.... playing the piano
.... reading
.... watching baseball
.... going to art exhibitions
.... cooking
.... playing cards

  B Listen to five short conversations (1–5) and identify the leisure activity that is being discussed in each conversation. Listen again and add any keywords that are missing from your list.

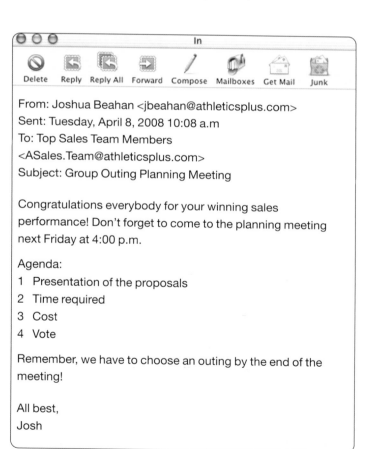

From: Joshua Beahan <jbeahan@athleticsplus.com>
Sent: Tuesday, April 8, 2008 10:08 a.m
To: Top Sales Team Members
<ASales.Team@athleticsplus.com>
Subject: Group Outing Planning Meeting

Congratulations everybody for your winning sales performance! Don't forget to come to the planning meeting next Friday at 4:00 p.m.

Agenda:
1 Presentation of the proposals
2 Time required
3 Cost
4 Vote

Remember, we have to choose an outing by the end of the meeting!

All best,
Josh

COMMUNICATION

You work for a major athletic equipment company. Because your sales team has exceeded the annual sales target, the company is financing a group outing as a reward. You have been invited to a meeting where you will propose an outing and try to convince the others to adopt your proposal. Choose one of the outings on page 171. Present to your group the advantages of the outing, the time it will take, and the cost. Once all the proposals have been discussed, your group must choose one.

8 Money

Snapshot

A Look at the pictures. Where are the people? What are they doing?

1

2

3

4

B Listen to the statements (A–D) and choose the one that describes each picture.

C Listen again and identify the verbs in the statements. Can you find a synonym for each verb?

	Verb	Synonym
1	....	....
2	....	....
3	....	....
4	....	....

DISCUSSION

What bank services do you use? How often do you go to your bank?

Listening 1

A Look at the chart showing the main sources of household expenditure. Place the items in the list below in the correct categories (1–12) in the chart. Write your answers in the blanks.

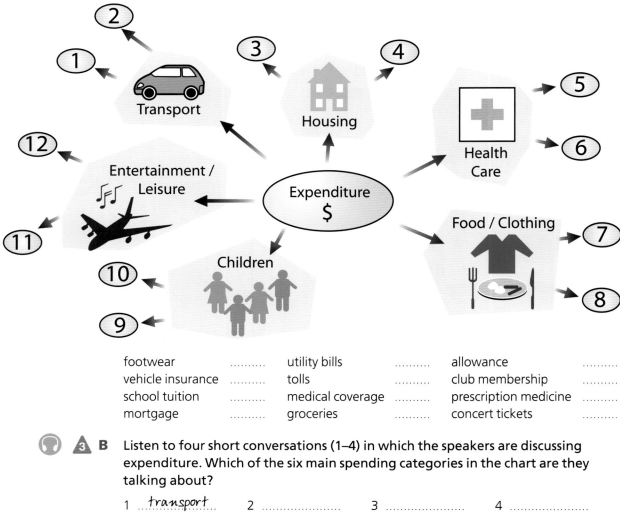

footwear	....	utility bills	....	allowance	....
vehicle insurance	....	tolls	....	club membership	....
school tuition	....	medical coverage	....	prescription medicine	....
mortgage	....	groceries	....	concert tickets	....

B Listen to four short conversations (1–4) in which the speakers are discussing expenditure. Which of the six main spending categories in the chart are they talking about?

1 ....transport........ 2 .... 3 .... 4 ....

C Now listen again and write down the vocabulary related to personal finance.

⚠ TOEIC® Tip

Being familiar with common abbreviations will help you to identify the context of a question. *ATM*, for example, is an abbreviation of *Automated Teller Machine*.

CEO	Chief Executive Officer	MBA	Master of Business Administration
IT	Information Technology	R&D	research and development
mph/kph	miles / kilometers per hour	asap	as soon as possible
PC	personal computer	Inc.	Incorporated
PR	public relations	i.e.	*id est* – that is
HR	Human Resources	e.g.	*exempli gratia* – for example

* The full forms of these Latin abbreviations are not normally used.

Grammar Check 1

Talking about trends

A Read the short text and list five verbs in the text that refer to upward movement and downward movement.

Microfinance

According to the United Nations, one way to lower poverty levels is by supporting the development of microfinance. Microfinance enables village people in developing countries to borrow small amounts of money from Microfinance Institutions (MFI's) in order to set up small community businesses. In theory, microenterprises of this type allow their founders to increase their income, which in turn raises consumption and the general standard of living in the community. The number of MFI's has grown steadily from a handful twenty years ago to more than 7,000 today. They are now contributing actively to the UN's objective of reducing the number of people living on less than $2 a day by 50% before 2015.

upward ⬆

1 ...... *increase* ......

2 ....

3 ....

downward ⬇

1 ....

2 ....

In which list would you include the following verbs?

go up .....   fall .....   rise .....   go down .....

decrease .....   drop .....   decline .....

B The words *increase* and *decrease* can be used as nouns or verbs. Which of the other verbs in the two lists have noun forms and what are they?

C Find the prepositions in the text that:

1 situate the beginning and the end of a trend or period   ....

2 give precise information about the extent of a change   ....

● see page 134 in the Grammar Reference section

D Look at the following bar chart and graph. What trends do they illustrate?

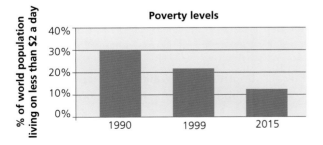

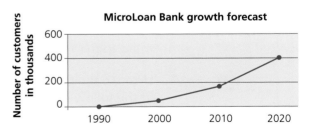

ACTIVE PRACTICE

Draw a simple chart / graph using the models in exercise D. Decide what your graph will represent (consumption – prices – employment – sales). Dictate the information in your chart / graph to another student.

6 **E** Complete the following letter from the president of the MicroLoan Bank with the appropriate words.

[1] *Reducing* global poverty is undoubtedly one of the greatest challenges that we face today. Although the proportion of those living in poverty [2]............... by as much as 5% [3]............... 1987 .... 2000, the number of people who still live on less than two dollars a day continues to [4]............... in many parts of the world. By [5]............... international trade and investment we can certainly alleviate some of this suffering. However, at the MicroLoan Bank we have always believed that it is only by empowering people, by enabling them to [6]............... their own standards of living, that we will ultimately prevail over poverty. Over the last ten years our bank's network [7]............... significantly and today serves more than 100,000 clients in developing countries around the globe. The United Nations millennium development target is to cut the number of people living in absolute poverty [8]............... 50% between now and the year 2015 – in simple terms that will mean achieving a [9]............... of one billion in the number of poor people over the next few years. However daunting that challenge may seem, it is my belief, and that of all the staff and volunteers here at the MicroLoan Bank, that we can and will succeed. The condition for that success is quite simple: individuals and businesses must [10]............... their commitment and support for this most fundamental cause.

Louise Bremner

PRESIDENT MICROLOAN BANK

 **TOEIC® Tip**

Watch out for the different words that can refer to numbers or amounts!

a dozen = 12	half a dozen = 6	a score = 20
zero = 0	"oh" = 0	double = x 2

Fractions/percentages   one half = 50%, one third = 33%, one quarter = 25%, one fifth = 20%, etc.

Decimals   one point five = 1.5

Multiple units   a pair, a couple, a trio, a quartet, duplicate, triplicate

Periods of time   a quarter = three months, a decade = ten years a century = 100 years

Frequency   once   twice

Listening 2

MoneyTalk is a weekly radio program where listeners can call in for advice on how to deal with personal finance problems. This week's show is about increasing your income.

 2 A Listen to the five calls (A–E) that Ed Jackson, the MoneyTalk host, receives. Which of the following topics does each caller ask about?

1	the stock market ....D....	4	selling a property	....
2	inheritance	....	5	pay	....
3	retirement	....			

B Listen again and note down the words related to income.

Vocabulary Builder

Phrasal verbs: two-part

Adding a preposition or adverb to a verb can change its meaning. Verbs of this type are called "phrasal verbs".

HAS YOUR CAR ¹BROKEN DOWN?

DO YOU NEED TO ²CARRY OUT EMERGENCY REPAIRS TO YOUR HOME?

³Take out insurance coverage under our new Home Protection policy and our professional services will be on hand 24 hours a day to ⁴deal with those difficult moments.

Just call your local branch and an advisor will ⁵go through the benefits and give you a quote.

A Look at the advertisement. Which of the verbs (1–5) could be replaced by the following synonyms or definitions?

make purchase handle discuss / explain had mechanical problems

B Combine the verbs in box 1 with an adverb or preposition from box 2 to form phrasal verbs. Then replace the verbs in bold in the sentences below.

1

bring	look	take
turn	set	work

2

after	down	forward
out	up	

1 I'd like to **withdraw** ...*take out*... $500 please.
2 So, how many people **responded to** .... our offer of free checking?
3 I still can't **understand** .... why my bank has charged me extra on my overdraft.
4 Mr. Lu is the person who **handles** .... loan applications.
5 Mailmart has announced that it will be **introducing** .... a new online payment system in the fall.
6 Can you **check** .... the bank reference code in the directory?
7 The government has decided to **advance** .... the date for submitting tax returns.
8 The bank has **refused** .... my application for a loan.
9 The exact conditions are **explained** .... in detail in the contract.
10 You need to provide proof of identity before you can **open** .... an account.

C Choose two of the verbs from the list below. How many phrasal verbs can you make by combining them with the prepositions or adverbs from box 2? Use a dictionary to help you.

check	come	cut	fall	get	go
look	make	pay	put	run	settle

Viewpoint

A What do you think is the best way for people to learn how to handle their finances? Read the following article and answer the questions.

Cashflow 101

By Amy Wu
The New York Times

EVERY FRIDAY NIGHT, John T. Carr III arrives at Wendy's restaurant in Midtown Manhattan – not for a burger, but for a board game.

After a quick dinner, Mr. Carr and the other regulars play a game called Cashflow, spending at least three hours rolling dice, moving colored figurines of rats across a multi-colored board, and becoming pseudo-millionaires.

Mr. Carr is among a growing number of Cashflow enthusiasts around the world. They are followers of the game and its creator, Robert T. Kiyosaki, known for his best-selling book *Rich Dad Poor Dad*.

Many players say the game gives them tools to gain wealth, helping them figure out ways to pursue their dreams by earning income beyond their nine-to-five jobs. Although many players have yet to match their game results with real life, there are Cashflow success stories.

One is Jay Feitlinger, 29, a Cashflow regular who quit his sales job last March. He and his wife, Rachel, bought a franchise of Aussie Pet Mobile, a pet-grooming business. Their goal is to net $100,000 this year. The Feitlingers regularly play host to Cashflow gatherings, and Mr. Feitlinger now is an occasional consultant to Mr. Kiyosaki's company.

Mr. Kiyosaki said he introduced the game in 1996 to help people better understand their finances. Up to six people can play the game. The first goal is to leave the rat race and move to the fast track, where players make money through investments rather than paychecks. Along the way, they acquire real estate, buy start-up companies, pay for children's education, and deal with problems like parking tickets and leaky water heaters. The first player to reach his or her financial dream is the winner.

"I think what he's done is very, very smart; he has recognized the consumer need to know how wealth creation works, and how people get rich," Eric A. Greenleaf, a marketing professor at New York University, said of Mr. Kiyosaki.

Critics of the game say that while it helps teach some basic financial skills, it may be more successful at creating illusions for people.

 B Match each question with a set of multiple-choice answers. Then circle the correct answer (a, b, c, or d) to the question.

1 Which of the following things has Mr. Kiyosaki not yet done?
2 What do the players have to do to win the game?
3 What job did Jay Feitlinger use to have?
4 What happened to Mr. Feitlinger last March?

............................?
a buy a franchise
b invest in mutual funds
c leave the rat race
d increase their paychecks

............................?
a written a book
b invented a game
c started a business
d opened a restaurant

............................?
a He got married.
b He became a full-time consultant.
c He left his job.
d He invested in a business.

............................?
a salesman
b consultant
c marketing professor/academic
d investment banker

DISCUSSION

Do you think playing games like Cashflow can really help people to become richer?

Grammar Check 2

Modals of possibility

A The modals *can, could, might, may, should, will,* and *shall* are used to express different degrees of likelihood. Look at their use in the sentences below. In which of the three categories (a, b, or c) would you include them?

● see page 134 in the Grammar Reference section

a Possible   b Impossible   c Certain

1 Customers **can't** withdraw more than $300 a day in cash. .....b....
2 It **can** take at least a month before a home loan is approved. ....
3 The insurance company **will** charge you for the whole year even if you decide to cancel after the first month. ....
4 To cash a check for more than $200, clients **may** be asked to provide ID. ....
5 It **could** be difficult to get your associates to agree to those conditions. ....
6 We **shall** need written confirmation of the transfer request. ....
7 You **might** find it more convenient to do your banking by phone. ....
8 The bank **won't** cover overdrafts beyond the specified limit. ....

B Read the sentences and choose the correct answer (a or b).

1 It .... take longer than two days to process your application.
   a couldn't   b shouldn't
2 We .... lend you an additional $1,000 if you maintain your credit record.
   a can   b won't
3 They've promised that all the paperwork .... be ready before next week.
   a will   b may
4 It .... be better to ask if you can repay the money in installments.
   a might   b shall
5 I'm afraid that we .... accept payment in cash.
   a can't   b mightn't
6 The local bank closes at six so I .... be able to get there in time.
   a can   b should

Listening 3

 Listen to the news report about the LETS system.
Answer the questions below.

1   What do the letters stand for?   L   ....

E   ....

T   ....

S   ....

2   Where was LETS invented?
3   How successful has LETS been?
4   What happens when you buy or sell inside a LETS group?

Communication

Your class is considering becoming a LETS group. Before you make the decision you have decided to organize an experimental session to see how it would work.

1   Each member of the class has been given a starting credit of 100 units of currency.
2   Each member of the class takes a piece of paper and writes a brief description of one item or service that he or she would be prepared to sell. (Example: CD collection – website design lesson – redecorating – chauffeur driving, etc.)
3   Form small groups. Discuss what things the members of your groups have to offer for sale and fix the prices that they will be sold for. Prepare a sheet of paper for your group with two columns. One column is for the purchases and the other for sales. Make sure that you leave enough space to write in the names of the group you will sell to or buy from. You will also need to write in the prices for each of the transactions that you make.
4   A representative of each group writes the list of items that their group is selling on the board.
5   Once all the goods and services have been presented, each group decides what they want to buy from other groups. Representatives from the group can then visit other groups to negotiate their purchases.
6   After a period of 30 minutes, each group prepares the final accounts for the trading that it has carried out.

DISCUSSION

Could this system work in real life? What would the advantages and disadvantages be? Would you like to participate in a LETS group?

9 Travel

Unit **Focus** · Tourism · Transport · Accommodation

Snapshot

A When was the last time you traveled? Where did you go?

B Look at the pictures and match each picture with one of the situations
listed below.

taking a cab	visiting a museum
clearing airport security	riding a shuttle bus
registering at a hotel	waiting at baggage claim
boarding a ferry boat	checking in at an airport

C Write a statement describing each picture.

Listening 1

  A Listen to three announcements (1–3) and then choose the best answer to the questions.

1 Who is the speaker in each of the announcements?

(1) ....   (2) ....   (3) ....

A a travel agent   D a customs official   G a hotel receptionist
B a flight attendant   E a train manager   H a catering manager
C a tourist guide   F a security agent   I a cabin steward

2 In which announcements do the speakers do the following actions?

(1) ....   (2) ....   (3) ....

A apologize for a delay   D welcome passengers
B describe an itinerary   E announce opening and closing times
C give details of dining facilities F invite passengers to fill out a form

3 Where would these announcements be made?

ACTIVE PRACTICE

Choose a favorite tourist destination from your country or region.
How would you describe this place?
What are the most interesting things to see and do there?
Prepare a description and then present it to another student.

Grammar Check 1

The language of obligation

A   Read the following text and <u>underline</u> the six verbs that refer to obligation.

Traveling

When you travel abroad there are certain regulations that you <u>have to</u> comply with; the immigration authorities in all countries require visitors to be in possession of the necessary travel documents. This means that they need to have at least a valid passport. However, depending on the country, they don't necessarily have to obtain a visa as well. Travelers must also be fully aware of the restrictions that apply to the goods that they are carrying. In some countries you must not import or export certain categories of goods such as plants, alcohol, or cultural artifacts.

Which of the verbs that you underlined are used to do the following?

● see page 135 in the Grammar Reference section

1   talk about things that you are forced to do   *must,*...............
2   indicate that something is not obligatory   ....
3   talk about things that you are not allowed to do   ....

 B   Read the instructions for passengers and complete them with the appropriate verb forms.

SkyWays AIRLINES

INSTRUCTIONS FOR PASSENGERS

Tickets

Passengers do not ¹...*need*.. a ticket when traveling on SkyWays airlines if they have made their reservations online. However, in order to complete our check-in procedures, all passengers ²............. provide check-in staff with both personal ID and their order confirmation number. Our check-in policy has been specially designed to ensure that you ³............ spend more than 30 minutes waiting in line and all passengers are invited to register at least one hour before their scheduled flight departures.

Baggage

SkyWays allows passengers 20 kilograms of checked baggage and one piece of hand luggage. If checked luggage weight exceeds the allowance, passengers will ⁴........... pay an extra charge of five euros per kilo. Hand luggage ⁵............ weigh more than five kilograms and ⁶............. fit into the spaces provided on the aircraft for underseat or overhead storage.

Passengers are reminded that they ⁷............. be able to certify that all their bags have been packed personally and that they do not contain any prohibited items. They are also advised that, as a result of new international security procedures, locked baggage may ⁸............. be opened by security personnel.

Special conditions

SkyWays Airlines flights may sometimes be overbooked and there is therefore a slight chance that passengers will be ⁹............. to accept seats on alternative flights.

If you have any doubts about SkyWays travel procedures, all you ¹⁰............. do is call our travel helpline at 0800 979 7979.

Listening 2

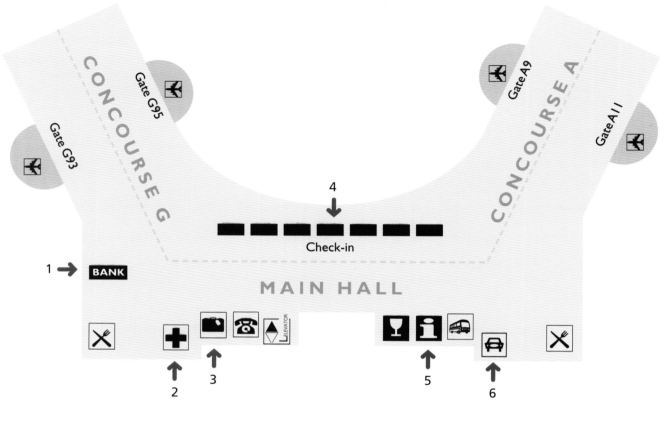

A Look at the floor plan of an airport terminal. Write the number (1–6) of where you would go if you:

had to change some money ....
needed to register for a flight ....
required medical assistance ....
wanted to rent a car ....
had lost a personal item ....
needed to find a hotel ....

  B Listen to three dialogues (1–3). In which of the six locations shown on the plan do you think these conversations most likely take place? What enquiries are being made?

	Location	Enquiry
1	....	....
2	....	....
3	....	....

Vocabulary Builder

Adjectives and adverbs

Adjectives can be formed by adding suffixes to words.
beauty – beautiful
marvel – marvelous

A Look at the list of other adjective-forming suffixes. Make the necessary changes to the words below, then add the correct suffix to form adjectives.

-able   -al   -an   -ant   -ar   -ary   -ate   -ent   -ible   -ic   -ive   -less

1	care............	5	origin...........	9	electron............
2	prime............	6	family...........	10	passion............
3	persuade...........	7	differ...........	11	access...........
4	reason...........	8	republic...........	12	observe...........

Adverbs can be formed by adding *-ly* to most adjectives.
beautiful – beautifully

B Which of the adjectives from the list above can be transformed into adverbs in this way?

Adjectives usually come before a noun but adverbs can be used either before or after a verb, or before a participle.
*Flight 465 is ready for **immediate** boarding.*
*All remaining passengers should proceed **immediately** to gate 16.*
*Discount tickets are not **immediately** available.*

6 C Read the following brochure and write in the correct form of the adjective or adverb.

⚠ TOEIC® Tip

Note that some words that end in *-ly* can be adjectives, adverbs or nouns.
*Toshiro flies **daily**.* (adverb)
*Toshiro takes the **daily** commuter flight to Sapporo.* (adjective)
*Toshiro reads a **daily**.* (noun)
Some words have the same adjective and adverb forms.
fast   straight   hard

Be careful – the two adverb forms of *hard* have very different meanings.
*She works **hard** (= she works a lot).*
*She **hardly** works (= she doesn't work very much).*

The Boca Negra Hotel and Conference Center offers one of

the region's most [1](*prestige*) .... venues for corporate seminars, sales conferences, and business retreats. Ideally located in the Sierra Pasada mountains, the hotel has [2](*panorama*) .... views and is within easy reach of MonteBello airport. The hotel's luxurious accommodations include 200 [3](*space*) .... rooms equipped with the finest furnishings and [4](*compliment*) .... Wi-Fi Internet access. A full range of [5](*recreation*) .... facilities, including an indoor pool and fitness center, is reserved [6](*exclusive*) .... for hotel guests. Our state-of-the-art conference center features multi-use meeting spaces, which can be customized to suit your [7](*profession*) .... needs. Our two main conference rooms can each [8](*comfortable*) .... seat 200 people and are paired with smaller meeting spaces. Both have the latest projection equipment, and our [9](*knowledge*) .... technical team is always available to ensure that your presentations are truly [10](*effect*) ....

For information or to make a reservation, please contact us at: resa@bocanet.com.

Viewpoint

 Read the questions and then skim the newspaper article for the answers.

TRAVEL DESK   **PRACTICAL TRAVELER**

Exotic Trips For Eco-tourists

BY MARTHA STEVENSON OLSON (NYT)

YOU'RE awake at four a.m., preparing to set out into the wetlands of the Okavango Delta of Botswana in search of the Nile crocodile, an efficient predator that grows to eighteen feet. It is your vacation, but you are part of a research team that checks crocodile traps to measure and weigh the reptiles, as well as take samples, perform tests, and tag them for identification. Halfway through the thirteen-day study tour, you will take the night shift, traveling by boat to conduct spotlight counts and capture smaller crocodiles by rope or by hand.

Such vacations – call them extreme eco-tours – are becoming more popular. They may be run in collaboration with scientists, with nonprofit organizations like Earthwatch, which has organized the crocodile study, or both. Some participants are looking for an exciting travel story and radical change of scenery; others are aware how fast pristine nature is disappearing and want to experience it firsthand. Many end up contributing their travel dollars and personal efforts to worthy environmental causes.

The comfort level can vary widely. Some expeditions involve sleeping on cots in tents or on mats in tribal huts; others are based at safari camps or hotels with every luxury.

Environmentally conscious and socially minded travelers should try to determine how much of an opportunity they will have to make a contribution at their destinations. Owners of eco-tour companies range from passionate idealists who want to aid conservation and local enterprise, to entrepreneurs riding a lucrative wave. Some nonprofit organizations offer tours where travelers pay a fee and enjoy the ride; others take paying volunteers who contribute their time and effort.

Adapted from *The New York Times*

"What fire? We're fleeing eco-tourists."

1   According to the article, what attracts people to eco-tourism vacations?

   a   Eco-tours are less expensive than package vacations.

   b   People are looking for a relaxing experience.

   c   Eco-tourists are concerned about preserving wildlife and its natural habitats.

   d   Local communities offer comfortable accommodation.

2   Which of the following groups of people is NOT involved in eco-tourism?

   a   scientists

   b   curators

   c   entrepreneurs

   d   volunteers

DISCUSSION

What do you think is the best way to discover a new country? Would you enjoy an eco-tourism vacation?

Grammar Check 2

Conditionals

A We use different conditional forms to talk about how likely situations are to occur. Look at the examples and answer the questions.

> 1 If she *takes* the 7:45 flight to Athens, she'*ll arrive* on time for the meeting.
> 2 When I *travel* to London, I always *bring* an umbrella.
> 3 If we *had* more vacation, we *would take* a trip around the world.

Which sentence refers to:

a future event that is not likely to happen? ....

a future event that is likely to happen? ....

a general state that is always true? ....

● *see page 135 in the Grammar Reference section*

Now identify the verb tenses in each of the examples in italics.

B Read some excerpts from a negotiation between travel agent Nancy Harper and Ignacio Lopez, manager at the Hotel Posada in Puerto Escondido. Fill in the blanks with the correct form of the conditional.

Nancy: Would you be able to provide conference rooms, if our clients [1](*to request*) ...*requested*... it?

Ignacio: We can host conferences if the group [2](*to include*) .... less than 100 people.

Nancy: If our clients wanted to book several rooms, what group rate [3](*to offer*) .... you ....?

Ignacio: If they reserve from five to nine rooms, they [4](*to receive*) .... a 20% discount. If groups [5](*to occupy*) .... more than ten rooms, then we'll offer a 30% special group discount.

Nancy: Would you be able to host large parties and family celebrations?

Ignacio: Provided that you give us advance notice, we [6](*to be able to*) .... accommodate all your needs.

Ignacio: If you can bring us 300 client bookings, then we [7](*to give*) .... you 10% commission.

Nancy: And if we [8](*to double*) .... that number of clients, what percentage would we receive?

Ignacio: Hmm. We [9](*to offer*) .... you 15% if you book over 500.

⚠ TOEIC® Tip

Look out for other words and phrases that express conditions.

They'll reimburse your travel costs *provided that* you submit the receipts.

We'll tour the gardens tomorrow *unless* it rains (= if it doesn't rain).

You'll receive a 20% discount on all car rentals *as long as* you show your membership card.

In case of fire, please use the hotel's emergency exits.

Listening 3

 Now listen to four other questions (1–4) that clients have asked Ignacio and choose the most appropriate response (A or B).

1 .... 2 .... 3 .... 4 ....

> Note that conditionals are commonly used in negotiations to discuss options and make offers. In negotiations, the first conditional is more direct and the second conditional is more polite and expresses more tentative offers.

Communication

Eco-tourism development

You are part of a planning team that is launching Amazon Adventures, an eco-tourism project that will be co-managed by members of a local community and by an eco-tourist developer. You are now in the final stage of negotiations. There are still three points that you must negotiate before reaching a final agreement.

Read the meeting agenda and prepare the negotiation for one of the role cards on page 172.

Members of the planning team:
Local Community Leader
Eco-tourism Developer
Eco-tourism Financial Investor
NGO* Representative

*NGO stands for Non-Governmental Organization.

AMAZON ADVENTURES

Agenda

1 Negotiate the number of eco-tourists to bring in every season.

2 Negotiate the duration of the contract.

3 Negotiate the distribution of profits.

4 Reach an agreement.

Units 7–9

🎧 Listening Test

Part 1

> **Directions:** Listen to the four recorded statements for each picture. Choose the statement that best describes what you see in the picture.

1

2

3

4

Part 2

> **Directions:** You will hear nine recorded questions each followed by three responses. Choose the best response for each question.

5	A	B	C
6	A	B	C
7	A	B	C
8	A	B	C
9	A	B	C
10	A	B	C
11	A	B	C
12	A	B	C
13	A	B	C

Part 3

Directions: Listen to the two conversations and answer the three questions that are asked about each conversation.

14 What is the woman asking about?
A Ground transportation
B Hotel rates
C Flight arrival times
D Customs procedures

15 Who does the man probably work for?
A An airline
B A taxi company
C A hotel
D A travel agency

16 How often does the service operate?
A Every two hours
B Every hour
C Every twenty minutes
D Every ten minutes

17 Where does this conversation take place?
A In a bank
B In a retail store
C In a library
D In a real-estate agency

18 Why can't the woman pay by credit card?
A Her card is damaged
B The nearest ATM is out of order
C The store is not able to process the transaction
D Her card has expired

19 What is the woman going to do?
A Return some items
B Pay by check
C Withdraw some cash
D Check her bank account

Part 4

Directions: Listen to the two short talks and answer three questions on each.

20 Where is this announcement being made?
A In the train station
B At the baggage claim
C In the departure lounge
D On board a plane

21 Which gate should passengers report to?
A Gate 44
B Gate 32
C Gate 3
D Gate 17

22 What are passengers NOT allowed to do?
A Carry photo ID
B Board from the rear
C Present boarding passes
D Bring more than one bag aboard

23 Who is this recorded message intended for?
A Tour guides
B Museum visitors
C Security staff
D Gallery owners

24 What are the commentaries about?
A Historical monuments
B A company visit
C Temporary exhibits
D Artwork in the permanent collection

25 How can the volume be adjusted?
A By pushing the red button
B By pressing the arrow keys
C By locating a white sticker
D By entering a number

Reading Test

Part 5

Directions: Choose the one word or phrase that best completes the sentence.

26 If you're thinking of remodeling your home, why not consider .... a home improvement loan with City Mutual Bank.
A   taking over
B   taking up
C   taking off
D   taking out

27 Customers should .... read the small print before signing a contract.
A   care
B   caring
C   carefully
D   careless

28 The shareholders were .... by the company's poor financial performance.
A   surprise
B   surprising
C   surprised
D   surprises

29 The new e-ticketing system, ... was installed last month, is working well.
A   what
B   whom
C   where
D   which

30 If we .... more free time, we would take the river cruise.
A   has
B   have
C   having
D   had

31 All passengers are .... to present hand baggage for inspection prior to departure.
A   required
B   requiring
C   requirement
D   requires

32 Inflation has risen .... almost 3% since last year.
A   at
B   by
C   from
D   with

33 The stadium was very .... at last week's game.
A   crowding
B   crowd
C   crowded
D   crowds

34 .... you need any assistance, please contact your personal banker.
A   Would
B   Could
C   Should
D   May

35 Participants .... to bring any special equipment as everything will be provided.
A   mustn't
B   don't need
C   need
D   needn't

36 Your personal banker can .... your loan application within one week of receiving the completed form.
A   to process
B   process
C   will process
D   processes

37 Does anybody happen to know whose squash racket ....?
A   is that
B   is this
C   that's
D   this is

Part 6

Directions: Four words or phrases are missing in the text. Choose the best answer to complete each empty space in the text.

Questions 38–41 refer to the following letter.

Dear Madam,

In reference to our telephone conversation this morning, I would like to confirm in writing our reservation for two rooms in your hotel for four nights. We'll arrive on July 2nd and plan on leaving in the morning on July 6th.

We would be very .... in attending the town concert on July 3rd. Would you ....

38 A interest
  B interesting
  C interested
  D interestingly

39 A occur
  B take place
  C manage
  D happen

to know if tickets are still available?

Your website mentions that guests need to .... by 11 a.m.

40 A check up
  B check over
  C check out
  D check with

Can we arrange to leave our bags at reception and then collect them mid-afternoon before we go out to the airport?

We are also considering extending our .... by one night.

41 A stay
  B period
  C rest
  D travel

If we decided to do so, would we have to make a formal reservation now?

Thank you in advance.
Kind regards,
Kitaru Fukuyama

Part 7

Directions: Read the following texts and choose the one best answer to each question.

Questions 42–43 refer to the letter.

42 What is the purpose of this letter?
A   To replace a lost bank card
B   To introduce a new customer to the bank
C   To communicate a PIN (Personal Identification Number)
D   To issue a new bank card

43 What transaction can NOT be carried out with this bank card?
A   Transferring funds from several accounts
B   Taking out money at bank machines
C   Paying for merchandise
D   Checking the account balance

Questions 44–47 refer to the following article from a newspaper.

Incheon International airport is the latest symbol of South Korea's economic ambitions.

The $5.6 billion dollar project includes a passenger terminal, which is the largest building in the country. The airport is part of a long-term strategy to place the country at the hub of South East Asia's transportation and travel businesses. Economists are already forecasting that by 2025 Pacific Asia will have overtaken North America as the world's busiest region for air passenger transport.

The spectacular architecture of the airport buildings is just one of the attractions that it has to offer; equally important is the fact that the whole project has been located on what used to be part of the Pacific Ocean.

As a result the airport is far enough away from residential areas to be able to operate twenty-four hours a day, without the burden of noise complaints from sleepless neighbors. Incheon is also ideally situated, lying midway between the capitals of two of the world's major economies: China and Japan. Construction is scheduled to continue until at least 2020 with the addition of two new runways and a high-speed train connection to the capital Seoul, all of which will almost double the total cost.

Incheon airport has certainly already made an impressive debut by winning two consecutive annual awards from the Airports Council International for the Best Airport Worldwide. The awards are based on more than 100,000 questionnaires completed by travelers at 66 international airports.

Northern Bank
9854 Tower 5
Sheffield Plaza
Ontario K1B 2B3
Canada

Tel: 735-3587

February 19th

Dear Customer

Please find enclosed your new credit card. This new card will replace your current card, which will soon expire. Your personal identification number will remain unchanged. You can use this card to:
• withdraw cash from all ATMs displaying the SwiftTrans logo
• obtain detailed account information
• guarantee your personal checks
• pay for purchases at most major retailers
   Please be sure that you sign your new card and destroy your expired card. You are responsible for the safekeeping of your card and you should not communicate your PIN to other people. You should also take all reasonable precautions when withdrawing money from ATMs in order to make sure that your number remains confidential.
   You should report a lost or stolen card immediately by calling the following toll free number 777-9989.
   On behalf of the staff at Northern Bank I'd like to thank you for your continued customer support. We look forward to being of service to you in the near future.

Sincerely,

James R. Stevenson

Customer Relations Manager

44 Which part of the world is most likely to have the highest number of air travelers in 2025?
A   North America
B   South Korea
C   Pacific Asia
D   Japan

45 Where is the airport located?
A   In the capital city
B   Inland
C   On the coast
D   In the suburbs

46 What can inferred about Incheon airport?
A   Passengers prefer it to other airports.
B   Local residents are unhappy about the noise it generates.
C   Passengers prefer high speed trains.
D   It can only be used during daytime.

47 The word "burden" in line 3 of paragraph 4 is closest in meaning to:
A   support
B   allowance
C   income
D   problem

Questions 48–50 refer to the following competition rules.

Essay Contest Rules and Regulations

1 Essay contest applicants must be 18 years old or older.

2 Applicants must submit a completed and signed application form along with two copies of one original essay, not exceeding 1,000 words in length. Only one entry per applicant is permitted. Submitted essays cannot be returned.

3 Submissions will only be accepted by mail and must be the original work of the applicant. Submissions may not be based, in whole or in part, on any previously published work or on the work of any third party liable to copyright infringement.

4 Submissions must be received by June 1. Submitted manuscripts should be typed, in at least 12-point font, and simply bound or stapled in the upper-left corner of the manuscript.

5 The "Grand Prize Winner" of the essay contest will be announced on October 15.

6 The "Grand Prize Winner" has one year from October 15 to redeem the €500 cash prize.

48 Who can participate in the contest?
A   Anyone
B   Only eighteen-year-olds
C   Anyone eighteen and above
D   Anyone under eighteen

49 How long can the essays be?
A   Longer than one thousand words
B   Not longer than one thousand words
C   Not longer than five hundred words
D   Any length

50 Which of the following do applicants NOT have to do?
A   Submit their essay typed
B   Complete a form
C   Pay an entry fee
D   Turn in their entry by a certain date

10 Environment

Snapshot

1

2

3

4

A Look at the pictures. What are the main features that you can see in them? Make a list of four words that you would expect to hear in the statements about each picture.

🎧 ⚠ **B** Listen to the statements (A–H). They each contain at least one reference to something that appears in the pictures, but only four are accurate descriptions. Which ones are they?

DISCUSSION

What do you think would be the advantages or disadvantages of living in each of the places shown in the pictures? Which of the places would you prefer to live in? Describe the place where you live.

Listening 1

The weather

A Look at the pictures. What extreme weather conditions do they illustrate? What are the effects of weather like this?

B Match the following weather symbols with the weather conditions listed below.

1	2	3	4	5	6	7	8	9	10

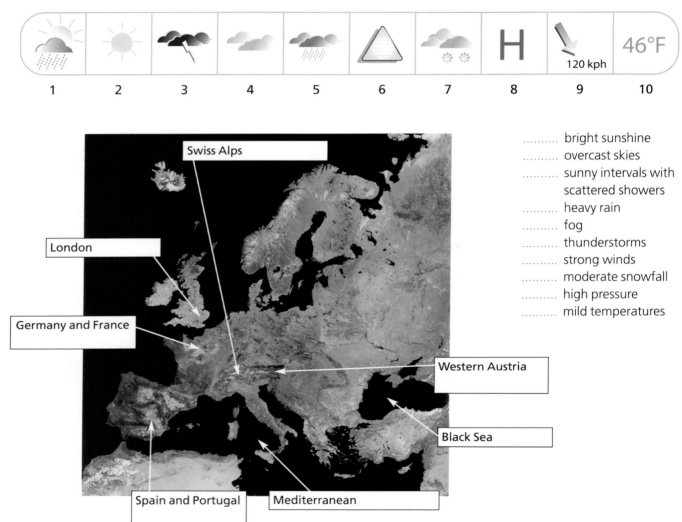

.... bright sunshine
.... overcast skies
.... sunny intervals with scattered showers
.... heavy rain
.... fog
.... thunderstorms
.... strong winds
.... moderate snowfall
.... high pressure
.... mild temperatures

4 **C** Look at the map and listen to the weather report. Write in the numbers of the weather symbols for conditions in each of the places shown.

DISCUSSION

How does the weather vary throughout the year in your country? How does it affect your daily routine? What is your favorite type of weather?

Grammar Check 1

Indirect speech

We use the verbs *say*, *tell*, and *ask* to report what other people have said.

A Look at the extract from a speech given by Lucas Sampieri at a conference on sustainable urban planning.

> *By mid-century more than 50% of the world's population will be living in cities.*

Now look at how the statement has been changed into indirect speech. What has been changed?

> Mr.Sampieri *said that* by mid-century more than 50% of the world's population *would* be living in cities.

B Look at the following question asked by a member of the audience.

> *Do you believe that technology is the best approach to urban development?*

Now look at this question transformed into indirect speech. How has the question been changed?

see page 135 in the Grammar Reference section

> A member of the audience *asked* M. Sampieri *if* he *believed* that technology *was* the best approach.

6 C Read the following extract from a report on M. Sampieri's speech. Choose the words that correctly complete the text.

M. Sampieri [1](*said / told*) that many cities in the world lacked the financial resources to invest in infrastructure. He [2](*asks / asked*) whether anyone in the audience [3](*will / would*) be willing to give up driving a car and ride a bike instead. He [4](*told / said*) the audience that some countries had already developed stricter development policies and went on [5](*to say / to tell*) that, in his view, others would have to do the same. He [6](*asked / told*) the delegates that sustainable urban development was the only way forward. He concluded by [7](*saying / telling*) that he [8](*has / had*) expected greater media coverage of the issue.

⚠ TOEIC® Tip

The verbs *say* and *tell* are easily confused.
When we use *say*, we don't refer to the person or people who is / are being addressed.
*The mayor **said** that investment in public transport would be doubled.*
Tell is followed by the person being addressed (except in such phrases as *to tell the truth, to tell a story*, etc.).
*Mr Coleman **told** the journalists that there would be a public enquiry.*
Tell is also used to refer to orders.
*The security services **told** the demonstrators to move behind the cordon.*

ACTIVE PRACTICE

Work in groups. Prepare a short questionnaire to find out what people think about climate change. Your questions should be designed to find out:

- if they are worried that climate change will affect them.
- if they have already modified their habits in any way to minimize the problem.
- what action they would be prepared to take to reduce climate change.
- whether they would be prepared to pay more for gas and for air travel.
- what factors are responsible for climate change.
- what the most serious consequences of climate change will be.

In pairs, interview each other using your questionnaires and then report your findings back to the group.

Viewpoint

A What is the capital city of your country like? How many people live there? How has it changed over the last few years?

 B Read the following article. Complete the blanks in paragraphs 1–3 with the appropriate collocations from the boxes above each paragraph.

City Limits

> carbon emissions   urban areas   ~~global warming~~
> road transportation

If governments do not act quickly to discourage the building of cities for cars, the international effort to control [1] *global warming* will become much more difficult, reports a new study by the Worldwatch Institute. Sprawling [2] .... are helping to make [3] .... the fastest growing source of the [4] .... warming the earth's atmosphere.

> parking lots   air pollution   new technologies

"Wind turbines, energy-efficient cars, and other [5] .... have received much attention in recent debates over energy policy, but we've been neglecting the role that urban design can play in stabilizing the climate," said Molly O'Meara Sheehan, author of *City Limits: Putting the Brakes on Sprawl*. "Local concerns like clogged roads, [6] .... , and deteriorating neighborhoods are already fueling a reaction against sprawl. Understanding the role of sprawl in climate change should only speed up the shift towards more parks and fewer [7] ....

> traffic accidents   recent research   physical exercise

[8] .... shows that sprawl already damages people's health. Each year, [9] .... take up to one million lives worldwide. In some countries, the number of lives cut short by illness from air pollution exceeds those lost to accidents. And by making driving necessary and walking and cycling less practical, sprawling cities contribute to weight problems by depriving people of needed [10] ....

By the end of the decade, the majority of the world's people will live in urban areas. Urban design decisions made today, especially in the developing world where car use is still low, will have an enormous impact on global warming. Adoption of the U.S. car-centered model would have disastrous consequences.

In thirty years, China, excluding Hong Kong, will have 752 million urban dwellers. If each were to copy the transportation habits of the average resident of San Francisco in 1990, the carbon emissions in urban China could exceed 1 billion tons.

"Some cities in developing countries have already proved that a strategy of de-emphasizing cars and providing public transit instead can work," said Sheehan. Starting in 1972, the city of Curitiba in Brazil built a system of busways and re-zoned areas along the thoroughfares – and is now enjoying better air quality and more parks for its 2.5 million people.

C List three things mentioned in the article that:

1 could help to reduce the threat of global warming.
   wind turbines ....

2 are negative effects of sprawl.
   ....

D Answer the following questions.
1 How many lives are lost every year in traffic accidents?
2 Which country will have a population of over 750 million people?
3 What will happen if China follows the U.S. car-centered model?
4 Which city has adopted a policy of reducing the use of cars?

DISCUSSION

What changes should be introduced to improve the lives of city dwellers?

Grammar Check 2

Reporting verbs

Read the conversation.

Have you seen the new development plans for the waterfront? They want to put up apartment buildings all along the river.

Yeah. I think it's a great idea.

I'm not so sure. A lot of businesses will have to move out of town.

When we report what people say, we do not use their exact words, but paraphrase, using reporting verbs. Look how the conversation is reported:

> They *disagreed* about the development plans for the waterfront. He *predicted* that businesses would leave.

There are three main types of reporting verbs:

a verbs followed by a preposition　　*She complained about* …
b verbs followed by an infinitive　　*They promised to* …
c verbs followed by a *that* clause　　*She predicted that* …

Which types (a, b or c) are the following reporting verbs?

 see page 136 in the Grammar Reference section

to admit	to promise	to advise	to agree	to announce
to apologize	to claim	to complain	to confirm	to propose
to disagree	to instruct	to invite	to predict	to warn

Listing 2

🎧 ▲₃ Listen to four conversations (1–4). Summarize them using reporting verbs.

1 *The man warned that the bus drivers would go on strike.*

2 ....

3 ....

4 ....

Vocabulary Builder

Idiomatic expressions 2: *make* and *do*

The verbs *make* and *do* are often associated with specific words or phrases.

> We still have to *make the arrangements* for the fire inspection.
> The urban planning commission has *done a study* of how commuters travel to and from their workplaces.

A Which of the two verbs is used with the following words and expressions?

1 ...*make*... the most of something
2 .... damage
3 .... your best, the rest
4 .... an impression, a difference, a change
5 .... work
6 .... something hard, easy, possible
7 .... the cooking, the ironing, the housework, the shopping, the programming
8 .... a mistake, an error, a miscalculation
9 .... a deal, business
10 .... money, a profit, a loss
11 .... a comment, a remark, a speech
12 .... use of something

6 B Read the text about how researchers at Robo Dom Co are developing systems for the home of the future. Use appropriate expressions with *make* and *do* from the list above to fill the blanks.

At Robo Dom Co, scientists are planning to [1] *make* a *change* to the way that the homes of the future will be designed. By [2] .... of a whole array of sensors, smart materials, and electronic devices, researchers think that it should be possible to get machines to [3] .... much of the .... that is required in today's homes. That should [4] .... it .... for overstressed urban professionals to save more precious time by handing over such daily tasks as [5] .... the .... or the vacuum cleaning to robotic servants. In exchange they would just have to spend a few minutes [6] .... the .... for the home computer system and then machines would [7] .... the .... Among other innovations, smart new soft kitchen surfaces would prevent you from [8] .... too much .... to your kitchen equipment and utensils when you're washing them in the sink. Smart containers will let you know when food inside is starting to deteriorate and automatic sensors in your fridge will inform you when it's time to go out and [9] .... some .... As a result people will be able to [10] .... the .... of their increasingly precious leisure time, that is, as long as their home operating systems haven't [11] .... too many ....

Listening 3

Living spaces for the future

The Freedom Ship is a project to create the world's first mobile, floating city where residents will own homes. In the following interview, Martin Kessler, a specialist on city environments, discusses some of the original ideas behind this project.

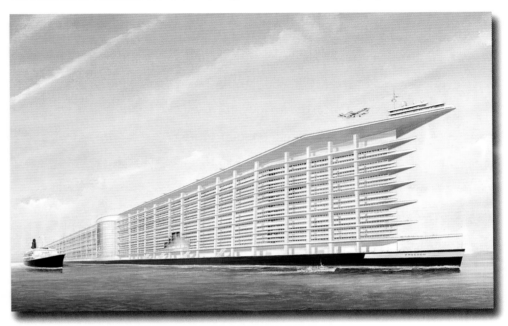

A Before you listen to the answers that he gives, read the list of questions that he is asked. How would you complete each of the questions?

1 .....When..... is the ship scheduled to be launched?   ....
2 .... kinds of people might be interested in buying properties
on the ship?   ....
3 .... will it cost to buy an apartment on board?   ....
4 .... are the advantages of living on board a ship?   ....
5 .... countries will the ship travel to?   ....
6 .... will people travel to and from the ship?   ....
7 .... facilities will be available?   ....
8 .... people can the ship carry?   .....A.....

 2 B Listen to the extracts (A–H) from the interview. Take notes about each of the answers that Mr. Kessler gives. Match each extract with the question it responds to and write the letters in the spaces above.

DISCUSSION

Would you like to live on board the Freedom Ship?

Communication

Winds of Change

Cape Cod is located in New England on the northeast coast of the United States and includes fifteen towns and two islands, Nantucket and Martha's Vineyard. The Cape is an extremely popular tourist destination and holiday resort and has a rich historical and maritime heritage. Its beautiful, virgin coastline of dunes and sandy beaches has made it one of the most sought-after locations for holiday homes and the area has some famous residences like the home of the Kennedy family at Hyannis Port.

N

Boston

Cape Cod

Hyannis Port

Martha's Vineyard

Nantucket

The Cape Cod community is currently facing a controversy; a group of electricity generating companies has announced a plan to install 130 wind towers at different offshore locations within six miles of the coast. This has created a debate in the local community, which is now divided between those who favor and those who oppose the development.

A discussion forum has been organized at which representatives of the various groups will be able to present their views on the project. Work in small groups. Choose a role card on pages 172–173 and use the information to prepare the arguments that you will use to support your case. Each group will then make a short presentation, outlining its position in relation to the development.

11 Health

Snapshot

1

2

3

4

A Look at the pictures. Which of the verbs below can be used to describe the body positions of the people in the pictures? Can you think of any other verbs to add to the list? Now make sentences using the verbs to describe the pictures.

kneeling	stretching	bending	lying down	leaning
balancing	holding	clutching	tilting	crouching

B Listen to the statements (A–H) and choose the one that best describes each picture.

Grammar Check 1

Gerund and infinitive forms

> A gerund is the noun form of a verb and ends in *-ing*: *examining, checking, consulting*.
> Infinitives are verb forms with *to*: *to examine, to check, to consult*.

A Look at the sentences below. Which verb is followed by the gerund and which by the infinitive?

1 Basketball is a sport that involves *running* and *jumping*.
2 They plan *to visit* mountain villages in Nepal.

● *see page 136 in the Grammar Reference section*

> After certain verbs, such as *involve, enjoy,* and *suggest,* we use a gerund form.
> After some verbs, such as *plan, agree,* and *decide,* we use an infinitive form.

 B Read the promotional letter and choose the gerund or infinitive that correctly completes the sentence.

Madison Health and Racquet Club
1421 MADISON AVENUE EAST • MIAMI, FLORIDA

Hello!

Do you enjoy ¹(*to play / playing*) tennis, squash, racquetball?

Would you like ²(*to attend / attending*) aerobics, tai chi, and yoga classes?

Like most health-conscious people, you have probably considered ³(*to become / becoming*) a member of a fitness club, but have put off ⁴(*to take / taking*) the first step because the fees were so high. But imagine ⁵(*to be / being*) a member without having to pay outrageous prices!

With Madison's new membership rates, you can afford ⁶(*to join / joining*) a state-of-the-art health club.

You can choose ⁷(*to work out / working out*) any day of the week between 6 a.m. and 11 p.m. And with over 100 machines, you will avoid ⁸(*to wait / waiting*) in line.

If you decide ⁹(*to sign / signing*) up within two weeks of receiving this offer, we promise ¹⁰(*to extend / extending*) your annual membership by one month! Act now!

We look forward to ¹¹(*hear / hearing*) from you very soon.

Best regards,

Stacey Sawyer

Stacey Sawyer, President and CEO

PS Don't forget ¹²(*to contact / contacting*) us asap at (555) 643-8000 or info@madison.club.com.

⚠ TOEIC® Tip

Use the gerund form after prepositions:
*After **swimming**, I feel refreshed.*
(never *After ~~to swim~~,...*)
and after verbs and expressions followed by prepositions:
*We're looking forward to **playing** tennis with you.*
*I'm interested in **learning** tai chi.*
Identify three uses of a gerund after a preposition in the letter above.

ACTIVE PRACTICE

With a partner, brainstorm a list of fitness activities. Which activities are most popular in your country? Now take turns interviewing each other about what fitness activities you like doing.

Do you belong to a fitness club? No, but I'd love to join one.
Do you do anything for physical exercise? Yes, I do weightlifting at the gym.
Do you like jogging? No, I prefer walking.

Listening 1

A Look at the list of health professionals. What do they do? Where do they work?

doctor

nurse

dentist

eye doctor / optometrist

veterinarian

surgeon

physical therapist

orthodontist

pharmacist

health insurance advisor

nutritionist

 B Listen to five short conversations (1–5) and write down two or three keywords from each.

Who is speaking? Where does each conversation take place?

	keywords	person?	place?
1	check-up, cleaning, molars, chew, X-ray	dentist	dentist's office
2			
3			
4			
5			

Viewpoint

A Make a list of the elements that you think are important for a healthy lifestyle. Now read the article and see how many of the things on your list are mentioned.

Living the Longer Life

Their grandparents live past 100, but the island's next generation may not make it to middle age.

BY Hideko Takayama

EVERY MORNING Seiryu Toguchi rises at six and exercises in the front yard of his home in Okinawa. He prepares a breakfast of rice and miso soup with spinach and egg. Then he tends his nearby farm, where he grows vegetables. At five p.m. he takes a hot bath and cooks home-grown radish with pork for supper. He reads newspapers, does his own laundry, and takes the bus to the nearest town when he needs to. It's nothing out of the ordinary – until you consider that Toguchi is nearly 102 years old.

Lean and fit, Toguchi jokes that his secret is a special drink he takes before bed: garlic, honey, turmeric, and aloe mixed with a local distilled liquor. His sharp mind and high energy may be rare among the elderly in other regions of the world, but he is not so unusual in this part of Japan. Indeed, Okinawa has the highest proportion of centenarians in the world: 39.5 for every 100,000 people.

What's their secret? In 2001, three specialists published a study of the locals' longevity in a book called *The Okinawa Program*. The authors found that elderly Okinawans had remarkably clean arteries and low cholesterol. Heart disease, breast cancer, and prostate cancer were rare, which they attributed to the consumption of locally grown vegetables, tofu, and seaweed, accompanied by rigorous activity and a low-stress lifestyle.

But increasingly, Okinawans are living more like Americans. That means less bean curd and walking, more burgers and stress. Only recently did Okinawans begin to recognize how the changes in diet and lifestyle were endangering their health. And it now seems unlikely that the island's children will live as long as their grandparents.

Doctors and government officials are urging Okinawans to return to their roots. *Ryukyu Shimpo*, the local daily newspaper, has begun a series of articles on longevity. "We want to give a warning to our people," says editor Takenori Miyara. "We will cover every area concerning our health situation, from history to culture, and from produce to what measures we should take."

One approach is to target the island's schoolchildren. At Johoku Junior High School in Naha, the lunches often include local dishes. "I like Big Macs, but I would rather eat more Okinawan food to stay healthy and live long," says Masatsugu Uemura, 15. The principal, Yayoko Ishikawa, says that Okinawans believed for decades that their lifestyle was scorned by the rest of Japan. "It has taken such a long time to realize what we had was a treasure for longevity," Ishikawa says. "We should start teaching our children about traditional foods and how the people lived." After all, few people know how to age well better than Okinawa's old folks.

B Look at the slides for a presentation about the Okinawa community. Using the article, make the necessary changes to correct the information presented in the first three slides. Write in the missing information for the fourth slide.

Slide 1

What makes elderly Okinawans so unique?

i they have unusually high levels of cholesterol

ii they are resistant to certain diseases

iii they get regular physical exercise

Slide 2

What foods are featured in the Okinawa diet?

i hamburgers

ii seaweed

iii fresh vegetables

Slide 3

Why is the younger generation in Okinawa less healthy?

i they have adopted Western lifestyles

ii their lives are less stressful

iii they get more exercise

Slide 4

What is being done to make people aware of the benefits of the traditional diet and lifestyle?

i ....

ii ....

iii ....

DISCUSSION

Describe your daily routine. What are the main similarities or differences between your lifestyle and that of traditional Okinawans?

Listening 2

  Before listening to the radio announcement, read the press release below. What information is missing? Listen to the announcement and fill in the blanks.

The United Okinawa Association

BASED ON WHAT DOCTORS LEARNED FROM A LANDMARK 25-YEAR STUDY OF THE WORLD'S LONGEST-LIVED POPULATION

THE
OKINAWA
WAY

HOW TO IMPROVE YOUR
HEALTH AND LONGEVITY
DRAMATICALLY

BRADLEY WILLCOX, MD, CRAIG WILLCOX, PhD
AND MAKOTO SUZUKI, MD

FOREWORD BY ANDREW WEIL, MD

The United Okinawa Association is pleased to announce that Bradley and Craig Willcox, the best-selling [1] *authors* of *The Okinawa Diet Plan*, will be speaking at a special evening event.

After hearing a short presentation of their research on the Okinawa community, you will have a chance to meet our guest speakers and to taste some of the unique [2]................. that they present in their book.

Join them at the [3]................. in Waikiki on May 15th from [4]................. until [5]................. and enjoy a fascinating and informative evening.

The $ [6]................. cover charge for the evening entitles you to your own hardback copy of their book.

Seating is limited, so book early if you don't want to miss this unique opportunity to find out about leading a healthier life.

Reserve now by calling 215-658-4321.

Grammar Check 2

Third conditional

> We use the third conditional to talk about what would have happened in a particular situation if conditions had been different.

A Look at the examples. Which part of each sentence is in the past perfect and which is in the conditional perfect (*would* + *have* + past participle)?

1 If I*'d had* an aspirin with me, I *would have taken* one immediately.
....

2 I *wouldn't have known* what to do if I *hadn't followed* a course in first aid.
....

● see page 137 in the Grammar Reference section

6 B Complete the gaps with the appropriate form of the third conditional. (You may need to use a negative form in some examples.)

Folk Medicine

If you ¹(*to live*) *had lived* one hundred years ago in America, you ²(*to have*) .... access to the same sort of medical treatment that people get from their local health centers today. And you ³(*to be able*) .... to run down to your local drugstore to pick up a pack of aspirin. You ⁴(*to have*) .... to rely on folk medicine and traditional remedies that had been handed down from generation to generation. But who knows whether those remedies ⁵(*to do*) .... you any good! Look at some of folk remedies that have been collected at the University of California at Los Angeles (UCLA). Which of these do you think⁶ (*to work*) .... the best and which do you think⁷ (*to be*) .... effective at all?

	Ailment		Remedy
1	Fever	a	bathe in vinegar and water
		b	put onion slices under your pillow
		c	apply an ice-pack
2	Headache	a	put a handful of salt on your head
		b	get your ears pierced
		c	lie down and cover your eyes with a wet rag
3	Sore throat	a	wear an old sock around your neck
		b	drink lime juice mixed with water
		c	eat a mixture of cheese, avocado and garlic
4	Cold	a	put a mustard plaster on your feet
		b	eat red peppers
		c	drink ginger tea
5	Insomnia	a	prepare a drink of warm milk
		b	put a horseshoe under your bed
		c	lie on your left side and wink with your right eye

C Tell your partner which remedies you would have chosen if you'd lived 100 years ago.

Listening 3

Giving advice and making suggestions

We use *should* and *ought to* to give advice.

> Before traveling abroad, you *should* check with your doctor to see if you need any vaccinations.
> You *ought to* renew your immunization against yellow fever soon.

Here are other phrases that are used to give advice and make suggestions:

> *Why don't you / we ...?*   *How about ...+ -ing?*   *What about ...+ -ing?*
> *Don't you think that you / we could ...?*   *If I were you, I would ...*

 As head of a planning committee for a regional health organization, Saskia Lindstrom is coordinating an annual "Vaccination Week". Read her memo, then listen to five extracts (A–E) from the planning meeting and indicate which item (I–V) they refer to on the agenda.

⚠ TOEIC® Tip

In Parts 2 and 3 of the test, listen carefully for question forms that make suggestions rather than ask for information: *Why don't you / we ...?, How about ...?, What about ...?* Note: *Why don't you call a doctor?* is not asking why you do not call, but is suggesting that you should call.

Memorandum

To: Members of the "Vaccination Week" Planning Committee
From: Saskia Lindstrom
Subject: "Vaccination Week" Meeting; Reminder and Agenda
Date: Friday 19 September

Dear Committee Members,

I would like to remind you of our next planning meeting:

Tuesday 23 September

9:00 a.m. – 4:00 p.m. in Conference Room C. Lunch will be provided.

Please look through the updated agenda before the meeting.

I look forward to hearing your suggestions.

Best regards,

S. Lindstrom

AGENDA

                                                     extract:

I   Identifying places to deliver the vaccinations   ......A......

II   Soliciting sponsorships & endorsements   ....

III   Involving the community   ....

IV   Devising the media communication plan   ....

V   Assessing the campaign's effectiveness   ....

Vocabulary Builder

Phrasal verbs 2: three-part

Some phrasal verbs are followed by an adverb and a preposition.

Read the article and match each <u>underlined</u> three-part phrasal verb (1–6) with its dictionary definition (a–f).

Physical Therapy on the Job

When occupational therapist Chip Wyler noticed that many of his company's skilled laborers were taking costly sick leave due to strain-related injuries, he discovered that many workers [1]<u>were</u> not <u>up to</u> the strenuous job requirements. So Wyler [2]<u>came up with</u> a unique stretch and flex pre-work program. Initially he [3]<u>ran up against</u> some resistance from management and workers alike. However, once he [4]<u>got through to</u> them that pre-work stretching would cut down on injuries, company support flourished. The 20 minutes of on-site productivity lost at the start of every work day is quickly [5]<u>made up for</u> by a 50 to 80% reduction in injury and compensation claims. Now, workers [6]<u>look forward to</u> doing the morning workouts and enjoying more injury-free days.

a | to experience an unexpected difficulty .....**3**.....

b | to feel pleased and excited about something that is going to happen ....

c | to replace something that has been lost, or to provide something good in order to make a bad situation better ....

d | to succeed in making someone understand or believe something ....

e | to be physically or mentally prepared for ....

f | to suggest or think of an idea or plan ....

Communication

Keeping the company healthy

MacroMix employs 2,000 staff at its headquarters in California. The Human Resources Director has recently conducted a survey to see how many work days are lost as a result of sick leave. The findings show that sick leave costs the company more and more money each year. Most of the absences are due to illnesses that are directly related to a lack of exercise, an unhealthy diet or poor stress management.

The HR director wants to introduce a new health program for MacroMix staff to reduce the annual sick days by 2%. Your team is in charge of designing the program.

Consult the role cards on page 173. Choose one area and present your findings at the team meeting. Then decide on the most cost-effective wellness program for MacroMix.

12 Society

Snapshot

1

2

Su Voto es Su Voz

3

4

A Look at the pictures and describe the people and places that you see. What is happening in the pictures?

B Listen to the statements (A–L) and choose two that best describe each picture.

Grammar Check 1

Words expressing contrast

The following linking expressions are used to express contrast.

but	although	even though	whereas	while	instead of
in spite of	despite	however	yet	even if	

A Study the sentences in the box below before answering the questions.

 see page 137 in the Grammar Reference section

1 Which words express contrast between two parts of the same sentence? ....
2 Which word is used before a noun phrase? ....
3 Which word shows contrast between two separate sentences? ....

> *Although* citizens have the right to vote, many do not take the time to register.
> *Despite* his excellent record, the governor lost the election to a newcomer.
> Legislators create laws, *whereas* the police enforce them.
> We wanted the referendum to pass. *However*, it failed at the polls by 6%.

B Combine the sentences using the words in parentheses.

1 The new candidate has less experience.
   I've decided to vote for her. (*even though*)

   ....

2 Some people like to vote in person.
   Others prefer using an absentee ballot. (*whereas*)

   ....

3 There were many observers monitoring the elections.
   There was widespread corruption. (*despite*)

   ....

Which other contrast words could replace those in the sentences (1–3) above?

6 C Choose the correct words or phrases to complete the voter's pamphlet.

U.S. CITIZENS LIVING OVERSEAS!

Did you know that you can vote in U.S. elections [1](*even though / yet*) you reside overseas? All U.S. citizens 18 years and older have the right to vote. [2](*Even / Even if*) you have never voted in the U.S. or have not lived in the country, your U.S. citizenship guarantees you the right to make your voice heard. You must first, [3](*in spite of / however*), register to vote and request an absentee ballot using the Federal Post Card Application. [4](*Although / But*) all states recognize the Federal Application, state guidelines do vary. Some states ask you to simply sign the application, [5](*despite / whereas*) others require that you sign the application in the presence of a witness or a notary. Your vote counts. Register today at: www.overseasvoters.com.

DISCUSSION

What are the voting policies and practices in your country?
Can a citizen vote from overseas by using an absentee ballot?

Listening 1

A Match the activities on the left with the corresponding places on the right.

voting	enforcing laws	taxation bureau	classroom
educating people	governing people	courtroom	police station
law-making	reporting income and paying taxes	city hall / capitol building	polling place

B Now brainstorm vocabulary related to the activities and places.

C Listen to five short conversations (1–5) and write down two or three keywords from each in the boxes provided. What activity is being discussed in each conversation?

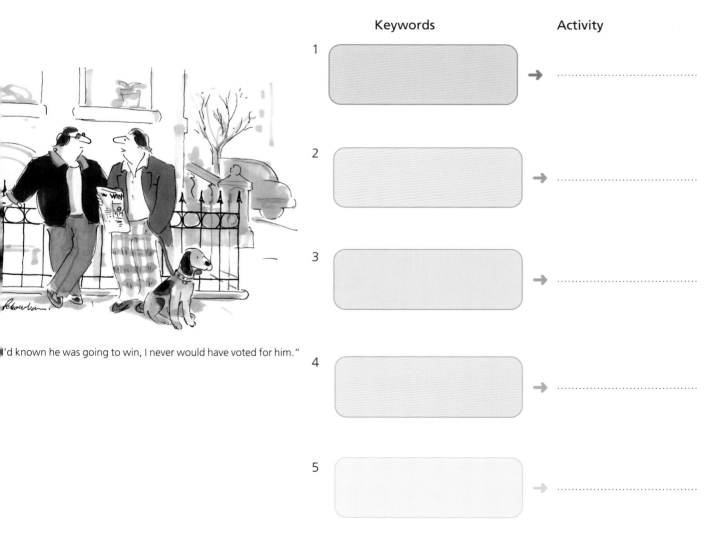

"...'d known he was going to win, I never would have voted for him."

Keywords   Activity

1 [ ] → ....

2 [ ] → ....

3 [ ] → ....

4 [ ] → ....

5 [ ] → ....

Vocabulary Builder

Collocations

Collocations are idiomatic word combinations.
Two common types of collocations are:

> Adjective + noun
> *a key factor, a unanimous decision, a vested interest, maximum security*
>
> Adverb + adjective
> *well qualified, highly recommended, cordially invited, strictly forbidden*

A Match each adjective with the most appropriate noun.

1	valuable	a	opportunity
2	golden	b	understanding
3	positive	c	collaboration
4	significant	d	lessons
5	close	e	contribution
6	mutual	f	attitude

B Now match each adverb with the most appropriate adjective.

1	highly	a	acclaimed
2	hugely	b	unlikely
3	critically	c	successful

C Read about George Dawson and fill in the blanks with seven of the collocations from above. Can you identify any other collocations within the paragraph?

Life-long Learning

George Dawson's extraordinary journey through the 20th century and how he learned to read at age 98.

Although it might seem [1] *highly unlikely* that someone would go back to school at the age of 98 in order to learn how to read, George Dawson is the notable exception. The [2] .... autobiography *Life is So Good* is the result of a [3] .... between George Dawson and school teacher and writer Richard Glaubman. In this remarkable book, George Dawson, a 103-year-old slave's grandson, reflects on the philosophy he learned from his father as he gives [4] .... in living and a fresh, first-hand view of American society during the 20th century. George Dawson's secret is his [5] .... – a belief that "life is so good." [6] .... by *The New York Times*, *The Washington Post* and many other literary reviews, *Life is So Good* makes a [7] .... to modern social history, offering insights into humanity, education and America. In the optimistic words of George Dawson, "Life is so good. I do believe it's getting better."

Listening 2

A Before listening to a talk about tribal law, read the following information about the Hopi Indian community.

Hopi Indian Reservation Key Facts

- The Hopi Indian Reservation covers more than 1.5 million acres.
- Old Oraibi, located on the Hopi reservation, is the oldest continuously inhabited village within the borders of the U.S.A.
- Hopi Indian villages operate independently from the U.S. federal government.
- The Hopi Indians have their own law enforcement, the Hopi Tribal Rangers.
- Hopi Indians are exempt from Arizona state taxes, but must pay federal taxes.

B Read the questions (1–3) and determine whether they are asking for general information or specific details.

1 Who is the intended audience of this talk?
   a students
   b law enforcement officers
   c government officials
   d lawyers
2 Why would someone attend this seminar?
   a to become a Hopi Tribal Officer
   b to work as a volunteer giving legal council
   c to learn how to translate Hopi language
   d to obtain legal advice
3 How long will this seminar last?
   a two hours   b a day   c three days   d a week

  C Listen to the talk given by a Hopi tribal council member and choose the best answer to the questions above.

⚠ TOEIC® Tip

Before listening to a short talk in Part 4 of the test, quickly skim the questions to determine what information to listen for. Stop reading before the recording starts, so that you can listen carefully for general and specific information.

DISCUSSION

Which countries have indigenous peoples?
Do they live in specially designated areas like reservations?
Do they speak a language that is different from the official language of your country?
What challenges do they face in their attempts to preserve their culture and traditions?

Grammar Check 2

Subjunctives: formal language in the U.S.

The subjunctive is the base form of a verb: ~~to~~ *have*
In U.S. English, the subjunctive is commonly used after verbs and adjectives when they are followed by *that* and express necessity.

● *see page 137 in the Grammar Reference section*

> The taxpayers **insist** that the governor **resign** immediately. (not ~~resigns~~)
> It is **crucial** that immigration quotas **be** respected.

5 Using the information provided on the Naturalization Home Page, complete the sentences with the subjunctive form of an appropriate verb in the box.

Welcome to the Naturalization Home Page

HOME

Naturalization is the process by which citizenship is granted to a foreign national. General requirements for naturalization include:

- continuous residence in the country
- proficiency in the national language
- knowledge and understanding of national history and government
- good moral character
- an attachment to the principles of the national constitution
- a favorable disposition toward the country

NEXT PAGE →

demonstrate	~~reside~~	understand	speak	be	show

1 The government requires that the applicant .....*reside*..... continuously in the country.
2 It is important that an applicant .... the national language.
3 It is desirable that an applicant .... national history.
4 It is necessary that the applicant .... of good moral character.
5 The naturalization bureau asks that an applicant .... a favorable disposition toward the country.
6 Immigration officials insist that an applicant .... attachment to the principles of the constitution.

⚠ **TOEIC® Tip**

In formal American English, the subjunctive is a common verb form and appears in Parts 5 and 6 of the test. Other varieties of English do not necessarily follow this rule.

DISCUSSION

What do you think about the citizenship requirements listed above?
Should proficiency in the official language be required for citizenship?
What are the naturalization requirements in your country?

Viewpoint

7 Look at the questions below and then read the article to find the answers.

to KILL an AVATAR

By Dan Hunter and
F. Gregory Lastowka

Norrath, the online world created by Sony, has more residents than Miami and a bigger gross national product than Bulgaria. Who will make its laws?

Although you know you are here, sitting at your computer, you are, virtually, "There". "There" is an online virtual world. The digital you is called an "avatar". Through your avatar, you seek out interesting locations, acquire virtual objects, and meet other avatars. "There" is one of the many virtual worlds where millions of people pay a monthly subscription to spend as much as 20 hours per week online.

Keeping a virtual world profitable means keeping subscribers' payments coming in, which means keeping subscribers happy. Like political leaders in the real world, game designers are under constant pressure from a citizenry with competing demands. Should a game stress equality among avatars or should it reward with greater power those who invest more time in the world? Striking the wrong balance could make the virtual world less attractive to new users or offend long-time subscribers. And designers must be mindful of avatars' freedoms. Part of the appeal of virtual worlds is the freedom they offer users. Each restriction may undermine the allure of the virtual environment.

Yet a major problem that has troubled virtual worlds from the start is crime. You might think that in worlds where avatars can fly and build their own castles, criminal activity disappears. But crimes have carried over from the real world to the virtual world, including fraud, theft, harassment, and virtual violence. One of the most prevalent is "player-killing". In virtual worlds, more powerful users can "eliminate" newcomers. Although the "death" of an avatar is generally not permanent, an avatar's being brought back to life is often time-consuming and expensive for the user.

If paying subscribers are constantly being murdered by bad avatars, subscriptions will surely decline, hurting the bottom line. When citizens complain about player-killings, some game designers have simply banished death by coding it out of the program. Like federal prosecutors, other designers have attempted to establish laws, but ultimately they do not have the resources to enforce them. As in the real world, online policing costs money, and it drives up the cost of subscriptions. Companies don't want "law and order," just profits.

You could make a virtual world without the possibility of crime – but would you have any subscribers?

1. What makes virtual worlds attractive to subscribers?
2. What are the arguments for and against allowing violence in online virtual worlds?
3. According to the article, what might happen if virtual violence is banned?
4. How are game designers of virtual worlds similar to politicians? lawmakers? police?

Listening 3

In debating, specific phrases have different functions such as:

asking for an opinion	requesting clarification	presenting an argument
agreeing	disagreeing	

A Match the underlined phrases below with the functions in the box.

1 I take issue with the idea that virtual violence promotes real-world violence.
2 Where do you stand on the issue of virtual violence?
3 Wouldn't it be better to offer a choice to subscribers?
4 I think you're right – parents shouldn't allow their children to play violent video games.
5 Are you saying that the government should restrict the sale of violent video games?

  B Now listen to four questions (1–4) and choose the appropriate response (A or B).

1 A B
2 A B
3 A B
4 A B

Communication

Debate: Should avatars in virtual worlds have the power to "eliminate" other players?

You are an active member of an online virtual world. A debate has been opened to discuss whether your virtual online world should allow violence. What laws, if any, should be established in your virtual world?

Divide into two groups:

Group A is FOR allowing violence.

Group B is AGAINST allowing violence.

Each group should first spend a few minutes discussing arguments before the debate.

Use ideas from the article *To Kill an Avatar* and the role cards on page 174 as well as debating phrases from Listening 3 to prepare your arguments.

Review Test 4

Units 10–12

🎧 Listening Test

Part 1

Directions: Listen to the four recorded statements for each picture. Choose the statement that best describes what you see in the picture.

1

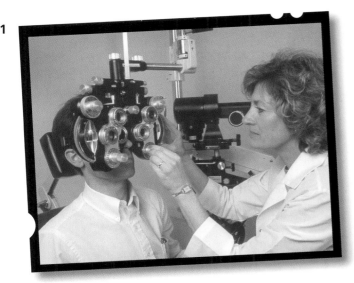

2

3

4

Part 2

Directions: You will hear ten recorded questions each followed by three responses. Choose the best response for each question.

5	A	B	C
6	A	B	C
7	A	B	C
8	A	B	C
9	A	B	C
10	A	B	C
11	A	B	C
12	A	B	C
13	A	B	C
14	A	B	C

Part 3

Directions: Listen to the two conversations and answer the three questions that are asked about each conversation.

15 What has the woman recently done?
   A   Rented an apartment
   B   Moved to another country
   C   Sold her house
   D   Purchased a home

16 How have prices evolved?
   A   They have risen significantly
   B   They have stabilized
   C   They have dropped slightly
   D   They have fallen sharply

17 Why is the woman leaving the city?
   A   There is too much noise
   B   It is too far from her work
   C   Property is too expensive
   D   Her apartment is too small

18 What is the subject of this conversation?
   A   Education
   B   Travel restrictions
   C   Work schedules
   D   Itineraries

19 When does Mary start work?
   A   At 9:00
   B   At 8:00
   C   At 10:00
   D   At 7:00

20 Where does the man go every morning?
   A   To school
   B   To the station
   C   To the store
   D   To pick up his children

Part 4

Directions: Listen to the two short talks and answer three questions on each.

21 Who would be most likely to attend this seminar?
   A   Employees
   B   Managers
   C   Aerobics instructors
   D   Doctors

22 What is the speaker recommending?
   A   That companies increase insurance costs
   B   That employees eat healthy food on-the-job
   C   That companies implement a health program
   D   That employees show greater loyalty

23 Which of the following would NOT be a benefit of the program?
   A   Less absenteeism
   B   Lower stress levels
   C   More positive attitudes
   D   Better opportunities for promotion

24 Why is this message being broadcast?
   A   To remind voters of state elections
   B   To alert drivers to road repairs
   C   To inform the public about school programs
   D   To warn residents of weather conditions

25 According to the report, who should be careful?
   A   Drivers
   B   School children
   C   Road crews
   D   Advisors

26 When will school begin tomorrow?
   A   At the normal time
   B   At 6 a.m
   C   Sixty minutes later than usual
   D   Classes have been cancelled

Reading Test

Part 5

Directions: Choose the one word or phrase that best completes the sentence.

27 Students must sign up for classes this week in order to avoid .... late fees.
A   paid
B   pay
C   to pay
D   paying

28 The weather service said that it ....
today.
A   is raining
B   rains
C   would rain
D   were to rain

29 Security measures are .... enforced on the premises.
A   suddenly
B   slightly
C   strictly
D   safely

30 The architect reported that they were .... progress on the condominium.
A   making
B   having
C   getting
D   doing

31 .... the candidate had more votes, he lost the overall election.
A   Even
B   However
C   Even though
D   Despite

32 We look forward to .... business with you again soon.
A   done
B   doing
C   does
D   do

33 If Steve .... his driver's license with him, the police officer would not have issued him a traffic ticket.
A   has
B   has had
C   would have had
D   had had

34 The hospital requires that each patient .... an admissions form.
A   complete
B   completes
C   did complete
D   has completed

35 The governor .... up with an innovative pollution reduction plan.
A   thought
B   came
C   let
D   found

36 Their lawyers feel that they .... to accept the settlement.
A   should
B   would
C   ought
D   had better

37 Before .... home, commuters are advised to check traffic conditions.
A   leave
B   to leave
C   leaving
D   left

38 The senior researcher .... agree with the findings in the environmental impact statement.
A   is not
B   has not
C   does not
D   was not

Part 6

Directions: Four words or phrases are missing in the text. Choose the best answer to complete each empty space in the text.

Questions 39–42 refer to the following announcement.

SCOTTSVALE PUBLIC LIBRARY NEWSLETTER

Scottsvale Public Library is celebrating its 50th anniversary with a special exhibition tracing the evolution of the local community from 1850 to the present. The exhibition was inaugurated on Saturday by Bill Hewitt, the Scottsvale mayor, who .... the audience that the library had

39 A told
   B spoke
   C said
   D asked

always brought Scottsvale's diverse communities closer together. "By giving everyone an opportunity to study, the library promotes mutual .... among our citizens, which in turn leads to the

40 A contribution
   B decision
   C understanding
   D attitude

enhancement of our community values," he said. .... the library is a non-profit making

41 A Although
   B Despite
   C Yet
   D But

institution, it does accept donations from both private individuals and corporate sponsors. Indeed, without the support of many generous benefactors, the library .... able to

42 A wouldn't be
   B won't be
   C wouldn't have been
   D isn't

acquire its unique collection of documents and photographs, many of which are on display at the exhibition.

Part 7

Directions: Read the following texts and choose the one best answer to each question.

Questions 43–45 refer to the following notice.

Renewal Notice

Drivers holding a State driver's license should apply for renewal of the license before it expires.

Licenses may be renewed as much as 90 days ahead of their expiration date.

The fee for a five-year license renewal is $25.

A $10 penalty will be charged if you renew your license more than 60 days after it has expired.

REMEMBER: driving without a valid license is against the law.

You can be issued a ticket if you are caught driving with an expired license.

---

43 Who would receive this notice?
   A   First time drivers
   B   People who have had their license suspended
   C   Drivers who have been issued a ticket
   D   Drivers whose license is about to expire

44 How much does it cost to renew a license?
   A $10
   B $25
   C $35
   D $60

45 According to the notice, how long are renewed licenses valid?
   A   Ninety days
   B   One year
   C   Five years
   D   Ten years

Questions 46–50 refer to the following web page and email.

Home | Information | Links | Contact us

Welcome to the Smart Business Recycling website

This site can help your business reduce the amount of trash it generates and throws away. These practices will save your company money, conserve landfill space, and protect the environment by preserving natural resources.

Use the **Recycler Finder** on this site to access more than 100 recyclers that reuse everything from bottles, cans, papers and plastics, to computers, concrete, textiles, tires, and wood. This site also includes industry-specific tips for reducing trash as well as case studies of businesses that have already successfully implemented waste reduction techniques. In addition, on the **Best Practices** page you

will find links to valuable websites and other resources to help you reduce your trash.

Our **Business Recycling Consultants** can assist you in setting up or expanding waste prevention and recycling programs by visiting your business and providing recommendations for **Reducing Your Waste** at no charge. To reach us for questions, comments, or to schedule a site visit, simply give us a call at (360) 532-6999.

If you're serious about running your business more efficiently by generating and disposing of less trash, then you truly are a smart business. Glad you joined us!

◄ Previous | Next ►

To: Smart Business Recycling
<contact@SBR.org>
From: ncastori@municipal.gov
Date: 8 May 10:03 PST
Subject: New Waste Management Guidelines

Dear Sir or Madam,
As head of the municipal Waste Management Task Force, I would like to applaud your efforts in helping us keep our communities green, safe, and healthy.
I am writing because I have studied your website and noticed that you do not include specific information about handling potentially hazardous waste materials, such as laser printer cartridges, batteries, etc. The Task Force has recently defined new guidelines for the proper disposal of such materials and is currently designing a new treatment facility. I would be more than happy to meet with one of your representatives in order to share with you these new handling, disposal, and treatment recommendations that you can then include on your website.

Looking forward to our future collaboration.

Best regards,
Nick Castori
Certified Engineer
Waste Management Task Force

46 What does this website give information about?
A Business opportunities
B Waste management practices
C Electricity savings
D Hiring techniques

47 Why should companies reduce trash?
A Landfills are empty.
B There's an abundance of natural resources.
C They would save money.
D Recyclers do not accept office equipment.

48 Which of the following is NOT mentioned on the website?
A Inviting a consultant to visit the company
B Checking the Best Practices link on the website
C Contacting the recommended recyclers
D Developing human resources

49 Who is Nick Castori?
A Director of Smart Business Recycling
B Leader of a task force
C Owner of a small business
D Webmaster of Smart Business Recycling's website

50 Why has he written the email?
A He's requesting more information.
B He's applying for a job.
C He'd like to supply additional information.
D He's enquiring about purchasing equipment.

Grammar Reference

This section includes further explanations of the main grammar points covered in the Grammar Check sections of the book.

Unit 1

Present simple and present continuous

The present simple

This is used to refer to:

- regular occurrences or actions that are frequently repeated

  I **take** the 8:15 train and usually **get** into work just before 9:00.

The following adverbs of frequency and time markers often appear in sentences of this type:

always	frequently	generally
hardly ever	normally	never
occasionally	often	rarely
regularly	sometimes	
systematically	usually	
once / twice (a day, a week, a month, a year)		
every (day, week, hour, month, year, time)		

- planned events and timetables

  The conference **opens** on Wednesday November 12th.

- events that are being described in a story or narrative

  He **goes** into his office, **turns on** the computer, and **discovers** that the file is missing.

- rules and written statements

  The contract **specifies** the exact number of hours to be worked.

- conditions in a first conditional sentence

  If she **gets** the promotion, she'll have to move to head office.

The present continuous

This is used to refer to:

- things that are taking place at the time of speaking

  Martha **is talking** to a customer on the phone.

- actions that have not yet been completed

  We **are training** the staff to use the new system.

- actions that are planned for a specific time in the future

  The auditors **are arriving** at ten.

- conditions that are temporary

  Juliet **is using** my office while I'm away.

Verbs in the present continuous are often associated with the following adverbs and time markers:

still	right now	at the moment
currently	at present	presently

Some verbs are never used in the continuous form:

~~Are~~ you ~~knowing~~ who is chairing the meeting?

Do you **know** who is chairing the meeting?

- verbs of cognition

  hear, know, believe, see

- verbs of feeling

  like, dislike, want, prefer

All other verbs have both continuous and simple forms.

Wh- questions

The following interrogative pronouns, adverbs and adjectives are used to introduce **wh-** question forms:

Question word		Refers to
what	(adj / pron)	objects, actions, states, people
when	(adv)	time
where	(adv)	location
which	(adj / pron)	objects, actions, states
who	(pron)	people
whom *	(pron)	people (indirect object)
whose	(adj)	people (possessive)
why	(adv)	actions, states
how	(adv)	actions, states

* Whom is mostly used in formal written English. In an informal context, **who** is more usual.

- Most **wh-** question forms are followed by an auxiliary verb and a personal pronoun:

  Why <u>did you</u> leave your previous employer?

What and who can be used as the subject of the verb. When this is the case, the auxiliary verb is not included and the verb is conjugated:

Who gave you my number?

- *How* questions are often formed with adjectives or adverbs such as *big, expensive, important, long, often, powerful, tall, wide:*

  How old *do you have to be to take early retirement?*

Some of the most common questions of this type are:

Duration	How long …?
Frequency	How often …?
Size	How big / wide / long / high …?
Age	How old …?
Degree	How powerful / strong …?

- *How much* and *how many* are usually associated with nouns:

  How many <u>people</u> *work in this department?*

Unit 2

Count and non-count nouns

Nouns are of three main types:

- count nouns. Most count nouns have plural forms with a final *s* or *es*:

a mistake	*some mistakes*
a watch	*the watches*

Some count nouns have irregular plural forms:

the woman	*the women*

Some of the most common irregular count nouns are the following:

aircraft	aircraft	child	children
fish	fish	foot	feet
man	men	person	people
sheep	sheep	tooth	teeth

- non-count nouns. They are only used in the singular. They are never used with the definite article *a* or *an*:

advice	*fun*

Some common non-count nouns are the following:

absence	anger	assistance
behavior	childhood	confidence
entertainment	food	growth
health	help	information
intelligence	knowledge	labor
luck	money	poverty
respect	safety	security
trade	training	transport
travel	water	wealth
welfare	work	worth

- nouns that have both count and non-count forms:

  My computer has already crashed two **times** *in the last 30 minutes.*

How much **time** *do we have for the presentation?*

Other examples of nouns that have both count and non-count forms are the following:

chance	experience	influence
power	time	youth

Prepositions

Prepositions of place

Prepositions of place give specific information about the position / location of one thing in relation to another:

The keys are kept **in** *a cabinet* **behind** *the reception desk.*

- The most common prepositions of place that are used to indicate static positions are:

above	across (from)	against	alongside
among	(a)round	at	behind
below	beneath	beside	between
beyond	by	close to	for
from	in	in front of	inside
near	next to	on top of	on
opposite	outside	over	to
under	underneath	with	within

- The following prepositions are used to indicate movement:

along	away	down	from
into	off	onto	toward(s)
through	past	up	

Prepositions of time

Prepositions of time give information about the timing or the duration of something.

Since *the position was advertised we've received 400 applications.*

The most common prepositions of time are:

after	at	before	by	during
for	from	in	on	since
through	to	until		

Unit 3

Articles *a, an, the*

The indefinite article a or an

The two forms of the indefinite article, *a* and *an*, are used with singular count nouns. (*An* is used before words beginning with a vowel, except when the vowel sound is *y* /j/.)

We use the indefinite article when we are referring to a noun in a general way. The indefinite article is not normally used with non-count nouns:

*A spokesman will be making **an** announcement later this afternoon.*

When we refer to nouns in a general way in the plural, we use the plural form of the noun (without an article):

***Mobile phones** are increasingly popular.*

When we want to be more specific we can use the adjective *some*:

***Some** viewers have complained.*

The definite article the

The definite article *the* is used before a noun or noun group (adjective + noun). It is used to refer to both singular and plural nouns:

- a specific person or thing

  ***The** Australian filmmaker, Jason Griffith, has been nominated for **the** award for **the** best* documentary.*

  * The definite article is always used before superlative adjectives.

- the names of institutions, organizations, and positions

  ***The** director of **the** Advertising Standards Authority has threatened to ban the campaign.*

- things that have already been mentioned

  *Is this **the** document you were looking for?*

- a general category

  ***The** press will be covering the ceremony.*

Non-count nouns are only preceded by the definite article when they are followed by a phrase or clause that gives specific information:

*The TV channels have **the** power <u>to influence public opinion.</u>*

Present perfect and past simple

The present perfect

The present perfect is formed with the auxiliary verb *have* plus the past participle or -*ed* form of the main verb (check your dictionary for irregular past participles):

*Our Internet provider **has** recently **upgraded** our connection speed.*

*The government spokesperson **hasn't** yet **made** a declaration to the press.*

We use the present perfect to talk about:

- events and actions that have started but are not yet finished

  *The number of viewers **has continued** to drop.*

- events and actions that took place at an unspecified time in the past

  *More than 10,000 people **have visited** our website.*

The present perfect can be used with:

- *for* to indicate the duration of something

  <u>We've used</u> digital technology **for** the last two years.

- *since* to indicate the starting point of a process

  *The new studio <u>has been</u> fully <u>booked</u> **since** March.*

The present perfect is used in the continuous form when we want to emphasize that a process has not been interrupted:

*They **have been working** on the problem all week.*

The present perfect is often used with time markers like:

already	almost	always	just
often	nearly	never/ever	yet*

* *Yet* is used with the negative and interrogative.

The past simple

The affirmative form of the past simple is formed by adding -*ed* to regular verbs or by using the past form of irregular verbs (again check your dictionary for irregular verbs):

*The unions **rejected** the government's offer.*

*Free FM **began** broadcasting one month ago.*

The interrogative and negative forms include the auxiliary *did*:

***Did** you listen to the news this morning?*

*No. I **didn't** have the radio on.*

We use the past simple to talk about:

- things that happened at a specific time or during a specific period in the past

  *The magazine **published** the article in December.*

- things that happened regularly in the past

  *Journalists **filed** their reports by phone.*

The past simple is associated with the following time markers:

after	afterwards	ago
before	finally	for
in	then	yesterday
last (week, etc.)		

Unit 4

Comparatives and superlatives

Comparatives

To make a comparative with one- or two-syllable adjectives, we add the suffix -*er*. With adjectives which end with the letter *y*, the suffix form is -*ier*:

strong	strong**er**
easy	eas**ier**

With adjectives of three or more syllables, the comparative is made by adding either *less* or *more* in front of the adjective:

*I think this model is **more** fashionable.*

Comparative adjectives are followed by *than* when we want to show what something is being compared to:

*Prices are low**er** **than** last year.*

We can also use *as … (adj) … as* and *not as … (adj) … as* to show the similarities or differences between two things:

*The packaging is **as** important **as** the design.*

*This model is not **as** powerful **as** the XP 80.*

Superlatives

To make a one- or two-syllable adjective into a superlative, we add the suffix *-est*. For longer adjectives we place *most* or *least* in front of the adjective. Superlative adjectives are always preceded by the definite article:

*Do you have **the** lat**est** model?*

*The Caribbean is **the most** popular destination at this time.*

The following adjectives have irregular comparative and superlative forms:

good	better	best
bad	worse	worst
little	less	least
more	more	most
far	further	furthest

Comparative adjectives are often preceded by one of the following words:

much	a lot	a little
significantly	slightly	

Tag questions

Tag questions are used in spoken English to confirm information, seek agreement, or express surprise or disbelief. Tag questions are made by adding an auxiliary verb and a personal pronoun at the end of a statement. When the verb in the first part of a question is in the affirmative, the tag question is in the negative and vice versa:

*You **take** credit cards, **don't you**?*

*The sales **don't** start until next week, **do they**?*

Unit 5

The passive

The passive is used when we want to focus on the outcome of an action or on the result of a process, and not on the people or agents that make it happen:

*Two prototypes **will be produced**.*

*The factory **is equipped** with robotic systems.*

When we want to include information about the agent in a passive sentence, we use the preposition *by*:

*The machine **is powered by** a small electric engine.*

The passive is formed with the verb *be* followed by the past participle. The passive forms of the main verb tenses are shown below:

Tense	Passive
Present simple	*Materials are delivered by truck.*
Present continuous	*Modifications are being made.*
Future	*The new version will be launched in June.*
Past simple	*The technology was invented in Japan.*
Present perfect	*Quality control has been improved.*
Past perfect	*The product had not been designed for extreme weather.*
Modals	*The testing should be finished next week.*

Causative verbs

Have *and* get

The causative verbs *have* and *get* are used when we want to indicate that one person caused another person to carry out an action.

Have usually indicates that the person used his or her authority to obtain the result:

*The plant manager **had** the electricians **rewire** the workshop.*

Get refers to a situation in which the person persuaded rather than ordered someone to carry out an action:

*The HR director **got** the workers **to accept** a new productivity agreement.*

Both verbs can be followed by an infinitive with or without *to* or by a past participle. With the past participle, it is not necessary to state who carried out the action:

*We've **had** the new procedures **certified**.*

*They **got** the vehicle **repaired**.*

Other causative verbs

Other causative verbs indicate differing degrees of authority or permission:

permission	*to allow, to let*
authority	*to force, to make*

The verbs *let* and *make* are always followed by an infinitive without *to*:

*Their supervisor **lets** them **take** one ten-minute break every two hours.*

The verbs *force* and *make* are always used with the infinitive with *to*:

*Machine operators should be **made to** wear full protective clothing.*

Unit 6

Future forms

Different tenses can be used to refer to future time.

The future

The future with *will* is used to:

- talk about things that have been planned or that are considered likely to happen

  *The goods **will arrive** on the 21st.*

- make general predictions based on normal behavior

  *Markets **will** always be volatile.*

- in conversation, to indicate willingness to do something

  ***I'll call** the customs office immediately.*

- in first conditional sentences

  *If we send the goods by air, it **will double** the transportation cost.*

The form *shall* is sometimes used in more formal contexts:

*We **shall confirm** our order in due course.*

When an event has already been planned, we very often use the continuous form:

*The ship **will be docking** at terminal B.*

going to

When we focus on people's intentions we often use *be going to* followed by an infinitive:

*They **are going to give** us a discount for the warehousing.*

The present tenses

When we refer to a future event that is part of a timetable or fixed schedule, we use the present simple:

*The first consignment **arrives** next week.*

When we are talking about an event that has already begun or that has been planned for a specific time, we use the present continuous:

*The Jakarta office **is closing** in January.*

The following time markers are used with the future:

after*	before*	by*
eventually	in*	in due course
one day	soon	sooner or later

* These words are followed by a reference to a date or point in time:

*The goods must be delivered **by** the end of the week.*

Cause and effect

When we talk about the causes and the effects of actions and events, we can use the following nouns, verbs and linking expressions. Note that verbs and nouns are usually followed by specific prepositions.

Nouns

Cause	Effect
the reason (for)	the effect (of / on)
the cause (of)	the result (of)
	the outcome

*The main **cause** of the crisis is reduced demand.*

Verbs

Cause	Effect
to result (from)	to result (in)
to cause	
to be caused (by)	to lead (to)
to be responsible (for)	to mean
to originate (from)	

Be sure to use the appropriate prepositions with these verbs:

*The lack of rain has **resulted in** poor harvests.*

*The current crisis has **resulted from** mismanagement.*

Linking expressions

Cause	Effect
since	as a result (of)
because (of)	thus
as	therefore
due to	so
	consequently

Unit 7

Relative pronouns: *that, who, whose, which, where*

Relative pronouns are used to give additional information about nouns. They are always followed by a relative clause containing at least one verb:

*Television is still the form of entertainment **that most people prefer**.*

Relative pronouns can refer to the following things:

Pronoun	Refers to
that*	people and things
what	things
where	places
which	things
who	people
whom*	people
whose	possessions

* *That* is only used in defining relative clauses.
* *Whom* is only used in formal written contexts.

Relative clauses

There are two types of relative clauses: defining and non-defining. Defining relative clauses give essential information about the nouns they modify:

*The player **who is the first to score ten points** wins.*

It is possible to omit the relative pronoun in a defining relative clause when the pronoun refers to the object of the main verb:

The show (that) we wanted to see was sold out.

Non-defining relative clauses introduce extra information that is not essential:

*Origami, **which originated in Japan,** is the art of making shapes from paper.*

A non-defining clause is always punctuated with commas and the relative pronoun cannot be omitted.

Indirect questions

Questions can be either direct or indirect:

What time does the show start? (direct)

***Could you tell me** what time the show starts?* (indirect)

In indirect questions, the word order of the second part of the sentence is in the affirmative form and does not contain an auxiliary verb.

The answers to indirect questions are the same as for direct questions except that they may be preceded by a response such as *Yes* or *No*, *Of course*, *Sure*:

Yes I could. It starts at 9.

Here are some other ways of introducing indirect questions:

***I wonder if** we could reserve a table for four?*

***We were wondering if** you'd be free to join us for lunch?*

***I don't suppose** you'd have time to meet this afternoon?*

***Would you happen to know** where I could get a taxi?*

***Do you know / have any idea** who won the match?*

Unit 8

Talking about trends

We use the following verbs and nouns to express negative (−) and positive (+) trends:

Verbs

transitive	intransitive
−	
decrease	decrease
reduce	
lower	
	fall
	drop
	go down
	decline
+	
increase	increase
raise	
	rise
	go up
	grow

Transitive verbs are always used with an object:

*The local utility has announced that it will **raise** the price of electricity by 2% in June.*

Intransitive verbs are never used with an object:

*Net income **has fallen** for the second quarter.*

When we want to describe significant changes, we can use the following intransitive verbs:

−	+
plummet	soar
plunge	skyrocket
slump	shoot up
collapse	

When we want to give the exact degree or duration of a change, we can do this by:

- indicating the beginning and the end of the trend with the prepositions *from* and *to*

  *The share price fell **from** $23 in June **to** only $12 in August.*

- using the preposition *by* to indicate the extent of the change

  *House prices have fallen **by** 3% over the last three months.*

Nouns, adjectives, and adverbs

The following nouns are used to describe trends:

−	+
a reduction	an increase
a decrease	a rise
a fall	a raise*
a drop	growth

* *A raise usually refers to salaries.*

The following adverbs and adjectives are often added to verbs and nouns to show the degree of change:

adjective	adverb
significant	significantly
sharp	sharply
slight	slightly
moderate	moderately

Modals of possibility

The following modal verbs are used to talk about possibility:

can	be able to
could	
may	might
will	shall
would	
should	
ought to	

- *can* and *be able to* are used in the present to talk about possibility

  We **can (are able to)** offer you a personal loan at 5%.

With the past tense, we use the forms *could* and *was able to* and with the future, we use *will be able to*:

  He **couldn't** remember how much he'd paid.

  We'**ll** never **be able to** afford the mortgage.

- *may* and *might* are used to talk about events that are considered likely but that are not certain

  The central bank **may/might** put up interest rates during the next quarter.

- *will* is used to talk about events that are certain to happen

  The local bank **will** be closed over the holiday period.

- *shall* is normally used for things that someone has decided to do

  I **shall** save as much as I can.

- *would* is used to talk about things that are certain to happen if particular conditions are fulfilled (see Conditionals)

  Prices **would** of course be affected if the weather conditions changed.

- *should* and *ought to* are used to talk about things that we expect to happen

  Consumer prices **should** rise more slowly during this quarter.

The modals *can*, *should*, *may*, and *might* also have past modal forms. We use these forms when we want to speculate or comment about past events:

  The finance ministry **shouldn't have published** such an inaccurate forecast.

Unit 9

The language of obligation

We use the following modal verbs to indicate obligation:

have to	must	need to

In most cases the three verbs are synonymous. However, there is no future and no past form of *must*.

Must is used to order somebody to do something:

  You **must** be ready to leave by five.

Have to expresses that something is necessary:

  I'm taking the night train because I **have to** attend a meeting at 9 a.m.

  I'**ll have to** call the travel agency and cancel the reservation.

  The captain **had to** ask for permission to dock.

The negative forms of the verbs have quite different meanings.

The negative forms of *need* and *have to* indicate an absence of obligation:

  You **don't have to** check out until 11 a.m.

However, the negative of *must* indicates that something is forbidden:

  Passengers are reminded that they **must not** leave their baggage unattended.

Other verbs expressing obligation are:

require	force	oblige

Conditionals

We use different forms of conditional clauses, depending on how likely it is that the event we are talking about will take place:

- if we are talking about something that happens repeatedly, we use the zero conditional with the present simple

  If / When I **have to** travel for business I always **take** my laptop.

- if the event is quite likely to happen but not certain, we use the first conditional with the present simple and the future tense

  I'**ll call you** at the office if my flight is late.

- if we want to speculate about a situation that does not exist at the time of speaking, we use the second conditional

  If I **had** the choice, I **would go** by train.

We can also use *unless* in a conditional clause. This gives the clause the meaning of *not*:

  We'**ll hold** the ceremony outside **unless it rains**.

If we start a conditional sentence with an *if* clause, we use a comma before the main clause:

  If I **had** more time**, I'd visit** the National Museum.

However, when we start a conditional sentence with the main clause, there is no need to include a comma:

  I'**d go** to the opera more often if it **weren't** (wasn't) so expensive.

Other words that often introduce a conditional clause are:

even if	whether	as long as	provided (that)

For information about the third conditional, see page 137.

Unit 10

Indirect speech

We use reported speech to talk about what other people have said. We do this by transforming what was said into a complete sentence in the past introduced by the verbs *say*, *tell* or *ask*.

The mayor's exact words, "The project has cost more than forecast" are expressed as follows:

  The mayor **said** that the project **had cost** more than initially forecast.

We transform the original tenses that were used by the speakers in the following ways:

present continuous	→	past continuous
present simple	→	past simple
past simple	→	past simple
		past perfect
present perfect	→	past perfect
future with *will*	→	*would*

Questions, instructions, and orders are reported with the verbs *ask* and *to tell*.

Questions

*The journalist **asked if / whether** the building would be completed on schedule.*

Instructions / orders

*The authorities have **asked / told** drivers **to** avoid using their cars and **to take** public transport instead.*

Say *and* tell

When we use the verb *say*, we do not have to indicate the person the message was addressed to:

*City planners **said** the new tramway will / would ease traffic congestion.*

When we use *tell*, we must indicate who the message was addressed to:

*Ms. Lopez **told the journalists** that the stadium would be inaugurated in July.*

Reporting verbs

Instead of reporting the exact words that a speaker used, we often paraphrase what was actually said by using reporting verbs. Reporting verbs are normally followed by different combinations of prepositions, infinitives or relative pronouns:

* verbs followed by *that*

   *The local residents **claimed that** the airport extension plan would cause house prices to fall.*

accept	acknowledge	add
admit	advise	agree
announce	believe	claim
complain	confirm	decide
disagree	discover	estimate
explain	feel	forget
hope	inform	insist
know	mean	mention
notice	persuade	predict
promise	realize	repeat
reply	think	threaten
warn	wish	worry

* verbs followed by *to*

   *The operators have **advised** rail travelers **to** expect delays of up to two hours.*

advise	agree	disagree	forbid
instruct	invite	order	persuade
promise	remind	urge	warn

Unit 11

Gerund and infinitive forms

Gerund

The gerund is formed by adding *-ing* to the base form of a verb.

Gerunds can be used in different ways:

* as non-count nouns

   ***Exercising** helps to keep you fit.*

* after certain verbs

   *The doctor suggested **changing** to a new diet.*

   *I dislike **working** with computers.*

   *Have you considered **following** a diet?*

Some of the other verbs that are always followed by a gerund are:

admit	adore	appreciate
avoid	delay	detest
enjoy	finish	imagine
involve	keep	mention
mind	miss	postpone
practice	recall	risk
stand	be used to	look forward to

* after the following prepositions

after	before	by	for
on	despite	without	since

The infinitive

The infinitive form is *to* + verb.

Infinitives are used:

* after certain adjectives

   *He was **unwilling to buy** her cigarettes.*

(un)able	bound	due
liable	(un)likely	

* in noun phrases that express purpose

   ***To reduce** your cholesterol, you should avoid fatty foods.*

* after certain verbs

   *The doctor **decided to refer** the patient to a specialist.*

Other verbs that are followed by the infinitive are:

| agree | intend | hope | plan |

Some verbs are used with the infinitive or with an object plus infinitive:

| beg | expect | help | want |

Other verbs are used only with an object plus infinitive:

| advise | warn |

Some verbs can be used with either a gerund or an infinitive:

Charles **likes <u>to do</u>** yoga.

Charles **likes <u>doing</u>** yoga.

With the following verbs, there is no major difference in meaning between the two forms:

| continue | like | hate | love | start |

But with the verbs *stop* and *remember* the meanings are different:

She **stopped <u>taking</u>** her medication.

(She doesn't take medication any more.)

She **stopped <u>to take</u>** her medication.

(She stopped what she was doing and took her medication.)

Third conditional

The third conditional is used to talk about what would have happened in a particular situation if conditions had been different:

If they **hadn't taken** an X-ray, they **would never have seen** that the bone was fractured.

Third conditional sentences have two clauses: the *if* clause always includes a verb in the past perfect, and the main clause contains *would* + *have* + a past participle (the conditional perfect). Either clause can be used to introduce a third conditional sentence.

Unit 12

Words expressing contrast

We use certain words to introduce a contrast between two statements:

While it is true that standards of living have risen, there are still large numbers of people living below the poverty level.

The following words can introduce a contrast between two clauses in the same sentence:

although	even if	even though
though	whereas	while
except that*		

* *Except that* is not used at the start of a sentence:

There is nothing wrong with the proposed legislation **except that** it will be difficult to apply.

Despite and *in spite of* are used before a noun or noun phrase and cannot be followed by a verb:

Despite the objections of some senators, the law was adopted.

However, *nonetheless*, and *nevertheless* introduce a contrast between two consecutive sentences:

Overall participation in the referendum has been higher than forecast. **However,** in some states only 30% of the population voted.

Subjunctives

The subjunctive is the base form of a verb without the preposition *to*. Subjunctive forms are used after certain verbs and adjectives and are introduced by *that*:

The government has suggested **that** the income tax threshold **be** raised.

It is essential **that** the new legislation **be** properly enforced.

The following verbs and adjectives are also used in this way:

- verbs

| ask | demand | insist | propose |
| recommend | request | | |

- adjectives

advisable	crucial	desirable
important	necessary	preferable
vital		

The subjunctive form is also used in formal English:

- with the verb *be* in a clause which begins with the word *whether*

Officers are requested to report all violations of road safety, **whether** they **be** serious or not.

- after *would rather* and *had better*

You**'d better register** soon if you want to vote.

TOEIC® Wordlist

As you progress through Target Score and prepare to take the TOEIC®, you can use the following wordlist to revise and review essential vocabulary. Next to each word write in: related terms, synonyms, definitions and / or examples that will help you to memorize and retain them.

machinery	50	site inspector	51
mail order	40	skill	11
mall	45	spare time	71
manufacture	47	special	74
medicine	112	spokesperson	32
membership	108	sponsorship	113
monitor	23	staff	11
mortgage	78	stake	58
neighborhood	102	standard of living	59
news bulletin	32	stationery	40
newsletter	30	stock	55
office supplies	21	stress	110
official	110	subscription	26
opponent	75	sue	23
outing	76	supervisor	15
overdraft	81	supplier	57
overseas	48	surplus	58
overtime	53	surveillance	23
paperwork	21	survey	31
parking lot	20	switch	30
pastime	70	tariffs	56
paycheck	82	taxpayer	120
performance	23	theft	121
plant	51	tourist guide	86
policy	81	tournament	71
politician	121	traffic	102
polls	116	training	13
pollution	102	travel agent	91
press conference	32	treatment	112
procedure	51	trip	90
raw materials	48	update	30
real estate	82	upgrade	30
refinery	51	utility	78
register	85	vacation	90
reliable	28	vaccination	113
requirement	120	volunteer	119
resident	102	wage	58
resort	106	warehouse	57
résumé	16	warranty	45
retirement	9	waste	51
sales clerk	45	waterfront	103
sales target	76	wealth	82
scenery	90	wholesale	55
schedule	15	wilderness	72
setting	73	withdraw	81
shipment	57	witness	116
shuttle	85	workforce	52
sick leave	114	workout	114

Audioscripts

1 Careers

Listening 1

A and B

1 **Man**   Hi Laura. This is Jason Jackman from ShowKase stores.

   Woman   Hi Jason. What can I do for you?

   Man   Well, I'm calling to ask you if there's any chance of getting Sabrina Marquez to do another contract with us. You know, she worked at our Lexington store last year during the holiday period. Is there any way we can get her back again this year?

   Woman   Just let me have a look at her schedule. OK, here it is. Well, right now she's working on a two-month contract for a department store. But that finishes on the fifteenth – when do you need her to start?

   Man   It would be great if she could start right after that and work through the end of January.

   Woman   She's down for another contract in January but that hasn't been finalized yet. Let me check with her on this.

   Man   I really need to get this sorted out pretty quickly. Can you get back to me before the end of the week?

   Woman   No problem. I'll let you know tomorrow.

2 **Woman**   PeoplePower. Can I help you?

   Man   Yes. My name is Howard Mason. I'm the HR manager of Dextro Logistics and we need to hire some temporary staff.

   Woman   Fine, Mr Mason. What exactly are you looking for?

   Man   Well I need to hire two truck drivers for a service contract that we've just taken on. Do you have any drivers available?

   Woman   Yes, we do have a number of drivers available. What does the job involve?

   Man   It's for an international assignment. We have to deliver some merchandise to a client in Mexico. And they gave us your name. The job would be for two drivers and would take about a week, I reckon.

   Woman   I'll need to know the exact dates and we'll also have to discuss the conditions and go over the contract together. I think it might be better to meet.

   Man   Sure. Could you come over to my office tomorrow mid-morning? We're at 19 West 57th, third floor.

   Woman   Just let me check. OK. That's fine. Shall we say at 11?

   Man   Fine. See you then.

3 **Woman**   This is Laura Alvarado of PeoplePower. Manfred Liebe, please?

   Man   Speaking. What can I do for you?

   Woman   Well, actually it's about Hamish Douglas, you know, the chef who's been working under contract with you for the last two weeks. I'm sorry to have to tell you this but he's just informed me that he's accepted a full-time position elsewhere without giving me any notice.

   Man   That's really a shame because he was working out so well. But I assume you'll be able to supply us with a replacement as soon as possible.

   Woman   Yes. I have a young French chef, Madeleine Legrand, who can replace him. She's just waiting for me to confirm the assignment.

   Man   This is a busy period and I can't afford to be short-staffed. Could you please have her call me first thing tomorrow?

Listening 2

A   What qualities make an ideal manager?
B   What is most important to you in a job?
C   How would you describe yourself?
D   What are your long-term career plans?
E   What are your present job responsibilities?
F   How do you spend your free time?
G   What skills have you developed recently?

Listening 3

B
Don Stanley

Good morning. My name's Don Stanley and I'd like to welcome you to my seminar "Getting the most out of the 15-minute interview." You know as recruitment managers, you may find that you have less time to spend interviewing. With more applicants due to Internet job postings and tougher competition for top prospects, recruiters have to be more efficient in the hiring process. Well, today I'm going to teach you some tips on how to do that. By following a few simple steps, you can save time without giving candidates the impression that you are rushing them through a quick and impersonal interview.

OK. First, open with small talk, but don't let it exceed two or three minutes.

Second, focus on a few essential questions.

Then, give the applicant a few minutes to ask questions about the job.

And finally, conclude by complimenting the candidate on their strengths.

So let me elaborate on my first point, small talk …

Kimberly Armstrong

At the end of most interviews, job-seekers have the opportunity to ask questions. But very few take advantage of this moment to learn more about the job. Remember, you also want to find out whether the company and the job are right for you. It's a good idea to ask what results are expected from the position. You may want to know how job performance is evaluated. You may also want to ask one or more of these questions:

"What are the challenges of this job?"

"What advancement opportunities can the company offer?" and "What are the long-term goals of this department?"

Questions like these can help you decide whether the job fits your career plans.

2 Workplaces

Listening 1

B

A Isn't there any way we can get the air-conditioning to work?

B Where am I going to put all these files?

C How can you concentrate with all that construction work going on outside?

D Don't you think they could provide more reserved spaces in the parking garage?

E Why can't they figure out what's wrong with my email account?

F Didn't the janitor say that he would get someone to clean the windows over the weekend?

G When are they going to turn the heating on?

H How come the conference rooms are always booked when you need them?

I Why don't you ask them to give you your own office?

J Can we close that window and keep the dust from coming in?

Listening 2

C

Welcome to my office. Yes, this is where I work. It may look like a mess to you, but don't worry, I know where everything is, or at least I'm pretty sure I do. As you can see I have a nice big desk where I can lay everything out, so it's usually covered with an assortment of things – reports that I'm working on, documents that I have to consult. There's an in-box tray too and you can just see it under that pile of papers. That's where I keep all the important correspondence that I have to deal with like invoices, bills and important emails I've printed out. Then there's the electronic heart of my working life, my computer, and I use it all the time. It's connected to a network and to the Internet and that's where I get most of the information I need. I have headphones too, so I can listen to music while I work.

On the wall behind it there are two shelves. The one on the left is where I put all the books that I need, you know, reference material, manuals, price lists, software guides and that sort of thing. And then on the one on the right, there's all my personal stuff like photos of the family and friends, and my collection of puppets. Oh, and also my two good luck charms – a silver key and a little miniature elephant. Under the desk you can just see a black filing cabinet. That's where I keep all the print documents that I need to refer to – reports and customer files. There's not that much in there because most of it's on the computer. It's also got a drawer where I keep all the office supplies that I need like staplers, tape, printer cartridges and so on.

Listening 3

B

A Man — Could you ask Mr. Walters to step into my office for a few minutes?

Woman — I'm afraid he's in a meeting right now. But he should be finished in an hour or so.

Man — Oh well, don't disturb him right now. But please tell him I do need to see him urgently.

B Man — I can't believe it. We don't have any instruction manuals left.

Woman — Why don't we call the Brussels office? They may be able to help us out.

Man — I've already done that. They're out of stock too.

Woman — So there's no way we'll be able to complete the order on time.

C Woman — Do you think I should apply for the management position in the customer service department?

Man — Well, you certainly have the experience. But it will mean working much longer hours and the salary's not that great.

Woman — I know. Maybe I'd be better off staying right where I am.

3 Communications

Snapshot

B

A The woman is mailing several letters.

B The keyboard is in front of the computer screen.

C   The mailbox is located on the sidewalk.

D   She's reading a daily paper.

E   There's a public phone next to the curb.

F   The woman is checking her email.

G   The newspapers are displayed in racks.

H   The woman is calling from a pay phone.

Listening 1

A

1   Woman   Would you happen to have any Italian newspapers?

    Man   I'm sorry. We usually sell out by noon.

    Woman   In that case, I'll take one of these magazines instead.

2   Man   Excuse me. I just heard my name being paged. Could you tell me where the nearest courtesy phone is?

    Woman   There's one in the baggage claim area over to your left.

    Man   Thank you. I hope they've found my suitcase.

3   Man   Should I mail the contract to Ms. Kim or can I fax it?

    Woman   Well, she'll need to sign the original so you'll have to send it. And you'd better hurry. The mail pick-up is in fifteen minutes.

    Man   No problem, it's all ready to go.

    Woman   That's great. That way she'll get it before the weekend.

4   Woman   It's almost seven o'clock. Are you going to watch the evening news?

    Man   I don't want to miss the overseas elections results. Which station do you prefer?

    Woman   Channel Five has the best international coverage.

5   Man   Do I have to type my log-in and password every time I want to check my email?

    Woman   Here, I can show you how to set your computer to do it automatically.

    Man   Thanks! That'll be a real timesaver.

Listening 2

B

A   That'd be great. I think he already has my number here at the office.

B   Hold just one moment and I'll connect you.

C   First dial 9 and then the number.

D   Yes, it is. How may I help you?

E   I can give you her cell phone number.

F   She won't be in till Monday. Would you like to leave a message for her?

G   Please do. That way everyone can hear the good news.

H   I'd like to speak to the department manager, please.

I   Please tell him that Mark Hunter called.

J   I'd like the phone number for radio station KZRK, please.

Listening 3

GloTelCom, the communications giant, announced it would be holding a press conference today at their local headquarters. Is the industry leader preparing to shut down local operations and move overseas? With quarterly profits down again, GloTelCom has union representatives and local government officials concerned that they may take more drastic measures after 1,000 skilled workers were let go two months ago in an effort to lower costs.

This comes only two weeks after the mayor said in a speech that the local economy was quote "strong and stable". If GloTelCom decides to reduce its workforce, the local economy and hundreds of families will be adversely affected. Moreover, the community has already seen many manufacturing jobs leave the area and according to union leaders, the future for local workers remains uncertain. It's unlikely laid-off workers would be able to find jobs in another factory.

Over the past fifteen years, the telecommunications industry has undergone enormous change. While most of the larger companies have already closed their domestic operations in order to move into cheaper labor markets, GloTelCom has remained until now, the exception.

Tune in at 3:00 p.m. for the GloTelCom press conference live.

Review Test 1 Units 1–3

Part 1

1   A   The men are moving the computers.
    B   They're walking through the office.
    C   The employees are lined up outside the office.
    D   They're seated at their desks.

2   A   They're working on a plan.
    B   They're tearing out the pages.
    C   They're painting a picture.
    D   The paper's folded in half.

3   A   The man's looking for his glasses.
    B   He's changing the tire.
    C   The man's standing beside the equipment.
    D   He's leaning against the truck.

4   A   He's mailing a letter.
    B   The man's behind the post.
    C   He's opening the package.
    D   He's delivering the mail.

Part 2

5   Why did you leave your last position?
    A   It lasted a little more than five years.
    B   I may have left it on the job site.
    C   Well, I went back to school to get an advanced degree.

6 When will we be able to move into the new building?
   A Just as soon as the lease has been signed.
   B I have a badge that allows me to enter the building at any time.
   C I think they're building a new movie theater.

7 I'd like a copy of today's paper, please.
   A Certainly. Would you like cream and sugar with that?
   B I'm afraid we've sold out.
   C I'm sorry. The photocopier is out of toner.

8 Don't you think there are too many commercials on TV?
   A I think she's coming in at the other station.
   B Definitely. I'm always changing channels.
   C Yes. Both men work in television advertising.

9 Excuse me, how far is the nearest post office?
   A Just around the corner.
   B They're close to completing the report.
   C It was posted on the bulletin board.

10 When did you hire the new restaurant manager?
    A It's much higher than we thought.
    B He started two weeks ago.
    C We're eating there next week.

11 How often is the outgoing mail picked up?
    A She picked him up on the way to work.
    B He often goes out in his pick-up.
    C It's collected twice daily, at noon and at six p.m.

12 Could you put me through to Mr. Takata, please?
    A He's on another line. May I take a message?
    B Please, take as many as you'd like.
    C Sure. You can put them here in the corner.

13 How did you find your new job?
    A I worked there for two years.
    B I answered an ad in the paper.
    C I need to sign the new contract.

Part 3
Questions 14–16:

Woman	The personnel manager has organized a training workshop this Friday.
Man	Yes, I heard. I'd like to go, but that's the day I visit my clients.
Woman	So do I. I wish they'd let us know about these events sooner.
Man	Yes. And I really do need some advice on how to improve my presentation skills.

Questions 17–19:

Woman	Who should we give the money to for Dr. Camara's retirement gift?
Man	Steve had volunteered to handle it. But since he's been transferred, Anita in the personnel department is taking care of it.
Woman	OK, I'll let all my colleagues on the research team know.
Man	Fine, just remind them that they only have until Friday.

Part 4
Questions 20–22:

Hello. This is Tonya Jackson in the subscriptions department of Business News publications. You recently subscribed to our magazine but the postal service has returned your first three issues of *Business News*. They've indicated that they are unable to deliver because the address listed is incomplete. Could you please call me back to confirm your home mailing address? The toll-free number is: 1-800-825-9838. Please accept our apologies.

Questions 23–25:

Thank you for attending today's opening ceremony for Somerset Business Park. The renovation of this historic industrial complex has created over 50,000 square feet of prime office space. Swanson Development remodeled four existing structures and added two office buildings to create a mixed-use complex, which also features a conference center and an indoor sports facility. Located only 15 minutes from downtown and the airport, the 150-acre business park is also fully equipped with the latest wireless technology, ensuring high-speed telecommunications and the most reliable voice, data, and video services. Tenants already include a major insurance firm and a leading information technology company. Congratulations to everyone involved. And welcome to Somerset Business Park!

4 Retailing
Snapshot
B
A She's purchasing some produce.
B He's giving her a refund.
C She's handing the woman her change.
D She's opening the cash register.
E They're setting up the market.
F She's arranging some items in the display case.
G They're returning the damaged goods.
H She's explaining how the TV set works.

Listening 1
C

1	Man	I'm looking for a birthday gift for my sixteen-year-old daughter. What would you recommend?
	Woman	Well, the embroidered designer jeans have been a big success with young people so far this season.
	Man	Yes I know, but she already has two pairs.
2	Man	Good morning. How can I help you?
	Woman	I'd like to know if it's possible to have all my purchases delivered directly to my hotel?

Man	Yes ma'am, we do offer a special delivery service. I'll just need your hotel address and room number.	
Woman	Oh, that's great. Is there any extra charge?	
3 Woman	When will you be receiving the new version of the game?	
Man	They're on order right now. So we should have them early next week. Would you like us to put one aside for you?	
Woman	No, thank you. I think I'll wait to see them once they're on display.	

Listening 2

Casa Camper

The Spanish design company Camper is on the move again. After successfully diversifying from footwear to food and restaurants, Camper is now venturing into a new sector of activity: hotels. The company opened its first hotel, Casa Camper, earlier this year in Barcelona. But Casa Camper is not just another hotel. It's a hotel with a lot of differences. Take the accommodation, for example: each of its 25 rooms has not one space but two: an elegant bedroom and an intimate lounge area where guests can relax or work. All rooms are equipped with Internet Wi-Fi and a plasma-screen television and there's even a hammock for that afternoon siesta. Guests also get 24-hour access to a free buffet with salads and snacks. Judging from the very positive comments that have appeared on travel websites, guests have welcomed the Camper hotel experience. Their only regret? That there aren't more Camper hotels to stay in. For that, they may not have to wait too long. The company has already planned a second hotel on its island homeland, Mallorca.

Listening 3

A We recommend that all drivers perform a routine inspection before they use their vehicles.

B Yes, that's right. Just leave us the full details of your address and we'll do the rest.

C No. I'm afraid we are not authorized to sell below list price.

D That depends. We advise drivers to check with the manager and to obtain permission before driving inside buildings.

E According to our estimates, it takes only 45 minutes to unpack and put together.

F Well, all new owners are invited to attend a 30-minute training session.

G That's right. If any part of the vehicle is defective, we replace it free of charge.

H Not necessarily. We only carry a limited number of items and we order all others direct from our supplier.

5 Industry

Snapshot

B

A The inspector is checking the equipment.

B They're working on an assembly line.

C The hot, molten steel is being poured into the mold.

D The holding tank is being tested.

E Shoes are being manufactured in the factory.

F The carpenters are wearing hard hats.

G The steel-worker is wearing protective eyewear.

H The structure is being built out of wood.

Listening 1

A Fortunately, delicious Jelly Belly beans are sold in over 35 countries worldwide.

B Jelly Belly beans are made in over 50 amazing and tasty flavors.

C Over one hundred thousand tons are produced every year.

D Our intensely flavored gourmet beans are conceived and tested by our experts in the Jelly Belly Research and Development Division.

E Absolutely! They were sent on the space shuttle in 1983 along with the first American female astronaut, Sally Ride! What a star!

Listening 2

A and B

A Woman	What seems to be the problem?	
Man	The pallets were run over by a forklift.	
Woman	You'd better file a damaged goods report.	
B Man 1	What happened to the safety screen?	
Man 2	It was taken off because it slowed production.	
Man 1	Have someone replace it immediately. We wouldn't want anyone to have an accident.	
C Woman	Excuse me. Hard hats must be worn at all times.	
Man	Oh, sorry. I seem to have left mine back in the truck.	
Woman	Here, you can borrow this one while you're on the site.	
D Woman	Has the faulty switch been repaired yet?	
Man	Unfortunately not. The warehouse can't seem to locate a spare part.	
Woman	Well, have the mechanic express order a new one. The assembly line needs to be up and running by tomorrow morning.	
E Woman	So, what does your analysis show?	
Man	The plant is not as efficient and cost-effective as it should be. We simply have to reduce labor costs.	
Woman	Perhaps we should invest in more automation.	

Man	That's probably the best solution. Robotics on the assembly line would allow us to increase production to 24 hours a day, seven days a week.

Listening 3

The mayor announced today that ancient ruins of an important settlement were uncovered two weeks ago by construction workers on the site of the new Metropolitan industrial park. Although an emergency archeological team has only begun exploratory excavations, a network of dwellings, remnants of a ceremonial area and burial grounds have already been located. Many domestic items have been unearthed and finely worked gold jewelry and small statues have also been found. University archeologists are declaring the site by far the most significant ever found in the region.

Not everyone, however, is celebrating. While the discovery has elicited praise from archeologists and local historians, it is also raising serious questions as to whether construction on the new Metropolitan industrial complex should continue. The archeological finds have seriously interrupted the construction of what was promised to be an enormous boost to local business. The planned industrial park would provide manufacturing facilities and office space for dozens of companies bringing in millions of dollars to a slow economy. A planning commission has been created to study all the options. Citizens interested in the future of the site are invited to a public meeting, to be held on Tuesday evening at the local Chamber of Commerce. The one thing that remains clear is that this site has been an attractive building area for hundreds, if not thousands, of years.

6 Trade

Snapshot

D

A The dockworker is directing the cargo.
B They're placing orders over the phone.
C They're bidding on the artwork.
D The harvested fruit is being arranged in rows.
E The traders are wearing vests.
F The auction house is crowded.
G The shipping container is being lifted.
H He's handling the produce.

Listening 1

A and B

1	Woman 1	Are we going to send the sculptures by air or ocean freight?
	Woman 2	With less than four weeks for transit, they'd better go by air.
	Woman 1	Right. That way they'll arrive in time for the art fair.

2	Man	Do you need any help with the packing list for this container?
	Woman	That'd be great, thanks. I was just about to inventory the breakable items.
	Man	Let's see. Five ceramic vases are designated as very fragile.
	Woman	Yes, and there are several antique bowls that have been specially wrapped.
3	Man	This drawing would make a fine addition to the museum's collection.
	Woman	And the reserve price is well within our acquisitions budget.
	Man	Let's begin bidding as soon as the auction opens.
4	Woman	Will all the paintings remain in the destination country?
	Man	Yes, we don't intend to re-export them.
	Woman	Then you'll have to pay your duty fees before departure.
5	Woman 1	Does this policy cover accidental damage to works of art?
	Woman 2	Yes, but you must provide a detailed list of all the pieces and their estimated values.
	Woman 1	Of course. We want to be sure that the entire shipment is completely covered.
	Woman 2	Here's the declaration form that you'll need. Please list all the items.

Listening 2

A recent study of the coffee industry has looked at the actual costs that make up the price of the coffee that the average American buys at the local coffee shop. Taking a cup of Starbuck's latte as the benchmark, the Specialty Coffee Association of America broke down the total retail price of three dollars and 75 cents into its component costs. The most expensive of those were; first the labor costs of staff employed at the outlet – that already takes a one dollar and 35 cent bite – then in second position the one dollar and 29 cents for store rent, marketing, and general administration. Add to that the 18 cents of interest on the shop owner's initial investment and the 25 cents of actual profit on each cup – and that already removes almost seventy percent of the full cost. Of the rest, the cup and the milk account for another 47 cents. So that only leaves 21 cents with 17.5 going to the middlemen; the exporters, the importers, the grinders. The farmers and growers who actually planted and harvested the coffee in the first place – end up with by far the smallest share: 3.5 cents.

Listening 3

A

1 Could someone take the minutes, please?
2 Has everyone received a copy of the agenda?
3 Could we move on to the next item?

4   What are your views on this issue?
5   Why don't we take a ten-minute break?
6   Is there any other business?
7   Who would like to chair the next meeting?

C

1   Could someone take the minutes, please?
   A   I'm sorry. I left my watch at home.
   B   I'd be glad to.

2   Has everyone received a copy of the agenda?
   A   You wouldn't have an extra one, would you?
   B   I've already had a cup this morning, thank you.

3   Could we move on to the next item?
   A   As soon as we've made a decision on the present issue.
   B   Relocating the business would be expensive.

4   What are your views on this issue?
   A   Yes, all rooms have lovely views of the city.
   B   I tend to agree with what Mark said earlier.

5   Why don't we take a ten-minute break?
   A   Because it's not broken.
   B   That's a good idea.

6   Is there any other business?
   A   No, I think we've covered everything.
   B   There're plenty of stores just down the street.

7   Who would like to chair the next meeting?
   A   I'll be happy to bring an extra one from my office.
   B   I'll do it. I think it's my turn.

Review Test 2 Units 4–6

Part 1

1   A   He's rolling up his sleeves.
   B   He's checking the pay roll.
   C   He's inspecting the roll of cloth.
   D   He's working on the clock.

2   A   She's pushing the grocery cart.
   B   He's weighing the vegetables.
   C   The customers are entering the mall.
   D   She's standing at the checkout counter.

3   A   They're waiting in line in front of the plant.
   B   They're attending a general assembly.
   C   They're walking around the new building.
   D   They're working on an assembly line.

4   A   The container is being lifted by a crane.
   B   The vehicles are being driven onto a ferry.
   C   The goods are being shipped by air.
   D   The truck is being towed away.

Part 2

5   When will the construction permits be signed?
   A   Within two weeks' time.
   B   Three days ago.
   C   By the local official.

6   If I place my order today, can I expect delivery before Wednesday?
   A   It's in the wrong order.
   B   It should get there by midweek.
   C   You should always follow orders.

7   Who'll be in charge of the auction?
   A   He's currently not available.
   B   Yes. The sale will begin soon.
   C   Tom Johnston will be managing it.

8   Which aisle is the pet food located in?
   A   I'm afraid animals are not allowed inside the store.
   B   At the far end of the store next to the canned goods.
   C   All our fresh fruit is locally produced.

9   Are you going to type up the minutes?
   A   Yes, I'm taking my watch to be repaired.
   B   I'll have my assistant do it.
   C   She's been tied up for hours on the other line.

10 This toy comes with batteries, doesn't it?
   A   No. I'm afraid they're sold separately.
   B   That's right. There is a ten percent service charge.
   C   The game can be played by up to four people.

11 Should we get subcontractors to finish the job?
   A   Yes, you can subtract the discount from the retail price.
   B   We'll save time if we do.
   C   The sublet has already been rented.

12 Would you like me to have the shipment insured?
   A   Yes. I'm certain I bought it here.
   B   Yes, it's much safer by sea.
   C   No. I'll take care of that myself.

13 How will they pay for the goods?
   A   In excellent condition.
   B   They'll transfer the money directly.
   C   Once they arrive.

Part 3

Questions 14–16:

Woman	Before we adjourn, would anyone like to add anything?
Man	We'll have to appoint a new committee chair before the end of the year.
Woman	That's right. I'll put it on next week's agenda.
Man	I'm afraid we won't have enough time to review the nominations. Let's schedule that for the meeting the following week.

Questions 17–19:

Man	When the container was opened, I noticed that water had leaked onto the fabrics.
Woman	You'll need to provide us with a detailed inventory of the damage and copies of the original invoices.
Man	All right. But how long will it take to get compensated?

Woman   As soon as you file your claim, we'll process it within two weeks. And depending on our assessment, you will receive payment within thirty days.

Part 4
Questions 20–22:

Now, if we could turn to the next item, which relates to new safety rules. The long-awaited renovation of our product research laboratory is set to begin next week. As of Monday, the north wing of the building will be designated a restricted-access construction site for the next six months. This means that in accordance with company safety regulations, unauthorized personnel will not be allowed into the site until the project is completed early next year. A memorandum has been issued asking company personnel working near the site to follow posted safety instructions.

During the final phases of the renovation, some of you may be granted access to the restricted area in order to oversee the installation of new laboratory equipment. This means that you will be required to attend a safety briefing and to wear appropriate protective clothing. For your own safety and for that of others, please pay careful attention to these new measures.

Questions 23–25:

The coffee industry has gone through a radical transformation in the last ten years and this has created some major problems for many coffee-exporting countries. The most important of these is the question of oversupply, which is the direct result of three factors; first, overall demand for coffee has in fact been declining. This is mainly because young people today tend to consume other products than coffee. Second, the International Coffee Federation, which used to guarantee that all producing countries were able to supply the market with sufficient quantities of coffee, is no longer able to act as the international regulator of the industry. And without a regulator it is impossible to impose maximum production levels. Lastly, in recent years, new countries like Vietnam and Brazil, for example, have entered the market, sometimes using extremely advanced, mechanized production techniques and this has led to the production of greater quantities of coffee, available at a very low price.

7 Leisure
Snapshot
B
A The men are playing pool.
B They're biking in the forest.
C There are a couple of free tables on the terrace.
D They're on stage performing a play.
E They're hiking in the wilderness.
F The men are playing board games in the pool.
G The players are on the field.
H The couple is dining outside.

Listening 1
B
How do Americans spend their free time?
Here are a few facts from LeisureTrak®, which measures the leisure and recreational habits of Americans 16 years old and over.
The top four leisure activities of all Americans are: watching television, reading, socializing and shopping. Using computers, eating out, watching spectator sports, and reading the newspaper also ranked high.
81% of Americans enjoy watching television at least once a day.
57% watch TV for less than two hours, but eight percent admit watching it for five or more hours per day.
The top five recreational activities for women are walking, aerobics, exercising, biking, and jogging. The top five for men are golf, basketball, walking, jogging, and biking.

Grammar Check 2
C
1 Would you happen to know where we can find a good restaurant?
2 I was wondering if you could make a reservation for two, please.
3 Could you tell us how the fish is prepared?
4 I wonder what today's dessert special is.

Listening 2
1 Would you happen to know what time the café opens?
    A No, I don't know what happened.
    B Yes, we're aware of that.
    C At quarter to twelve.
2 Could you please show me how to use these chopsticks?
    A Gladly. You first have to learn how to hold them.
    B Yes. We were all very pleased with the show.
    C No. She hasn't been able to show her work.
3 I wonder if anyone would like to go out for a drink this evening?
    A It's a wonder they're here.
    B Nobody won this afternoon.
    C We'd love to.

Listening 3
B
1 Man 1   I know a great place to play. The municipal recreation department has set up nice tables with nets in the park.
    Man 2   Well, what about paddles and balls?
    Man 1   We can rent paddles at the kiosk. We'll have to buy a few balls though.

2 Woman That was an amazing show. Over one hundred works in such a small gallery.

Man I found it very crowded. The paintings were hung so close together and the sculptures were packed into the corners.

Woman We should come back when there are less people. Until then you can read through the catalog that I bought on my way out.

3 Man How about that game last night! It sure was close in the last inning.

Woman You can say that again. If it weren't for Yuchiro's home run with bases loaded, we would have lost the game.

Man What a hitter! Not only is he a solid fielder, he can really swing the bat.

4 Man 1 Hey there. How've you been? Last time we met you had just signed up for an Italian cuisine class.

Man 2 Great to see you. Yeah. I've been taking my life-long hobby very seriously and just finished another six-month dessert and pastry course. It was fabulous!

Man 1 Wow. With all that experience you'll have your own restaurant in no time!

5 Man What a fine rendition. That was terrific. So how long have you been playing?

Woman I started taking lessons when I turned five. So, counting the conservatory, that makes about 20 years that I've had my fingers on the keys.

Man Do you mostly play classical or sometimes improvise jazz?

8 Money

Snapshot

B and C

A He's converting some money into another currency.
B They're withdrawing cash from an ATM.
C She's checking some sheets of dollar bills.
D The bank teller is assisting a customer.

Listening 1

B and C

1 Woman The garage called this morning. They said they've found a problem with the brake system on the car, which means they're going to charge us more.

Man Did they give you an estimate?

Woman Around two hundred dollars, including labor.

2 Man Why don't we get tickets for the opera festival next week?

Woman Have you seen what they cost? There's no way we can afford that much.

Man I guess you're right. Maybe we should just go to a jazz concert instead.

3 Man I'm looking for a small two-bedroom apartment.

Woman Well, we have one that's just been vacated. It's on Jermyn Avenue near the new sports complex.

Man That sounds great. How much is the rent?

4 Woman Can you believe that electricity has gone up again?

Man I figure it's increased by almost seven percent since last year.

Woman Yeah. I'm seriously considering switching to solar energy.

Listening 2

A and B

A My home is already worth about 140,000 dollars. Would you advise me to sell it now or would it be better to wait for it to appreciate?
B I've been at the same salary level for the last two years. How should I go about asking my boss for a raise?
C Is there an annual limit on the amount of money I can put into my pension fund?
D I'm interested in buying stocks. How should I choose which companies to invest in?
E I recently inherited some money. What type of investment would give me the best return?

Listening 3

LETS is the name of an open currency system which was invented by Cambridge University graduate, Michael Linton. Although the letters of LETS officially stand for "Local Exchange Trading System", the word LETS also serves as an invitation to people to exchange their goods and services in a different way. Back in 1983, when he first came up with the idea, Michael was living on Vancouver Island in Canada. There he noticed that while the local community had significant resources and plenty of skills and products to offer, little trading was taking place. Why not? Simply because there wasn't enough money circulating to make that possible. The solution? Create a "virtual bank" where users can trade with each other using their own virtual money to supplement whatever "real" money they have available. How does it work? Nothing could be simpler. It's just like a normal bank – except that there are no buildings, no deposits, hardly any staff and absolutely no owners. But there is money and it does circulate, even though it's actually only virtual money. All the transactions, prices and conditions are negotiated directly between buyer and seller, and payment is made by check or on-line transfer. In most LETS systems, users can see the general state of the system accounts but details are private. However, in others where there are trust / distrust issues, all accounting can be made open to all users. Sounds simple and it is – which may well explain why today you can find LETS groups in over 38 countries around the globe.

9 Travel

Listening 1

A

1 Welcome aboard. Today's river cruise is scheduled to last one hour. During the first part of our journey we will be sailing upstream, along the south bank. This will take us through the heart of the old city and up to St Michael's Island where you will be able to admire the city's spectacular medieval cathedral. After that we will return downstream, along the north side of the river past The Museum of Modern Art, the Exhibition Center and the magnificent Royal Palace and gardens. Now if you look over to your right, you'll be able to make out the green roof of the City Hall …

2 We regret to inform passengers that today's service to London Waterloo will be subject to delays due to a malfunction of the signalling systems. Our arrival time will now be 11:45, two hours later than scheduled. On behalf of Eurotrains we would like to apologize for the inconvenience and we would like to remind passengers that they are entitled to a partial refund of their fares on completion of the forms that our personnel will distribute on arrival at the station.

3 We would like to inform all passengers sailing with Sea / Ocean Ferries that our self-service and *à la carte* restaurants are now open for dining. Our self-service restaurant, which is located on B deck, offers a wide selection of local and international dishes. It closes at 11 p.m. Our *à la carte* restaurant, The Wheelhouse, is situated on the upper deck and offers a gourmet dining experience with spectacular sea views. Reservations will be accepted until 10 p.m.

Listening 2

B

1	Woman	Could you recommend a nice hotel near the convention center?
	Man	Try the Hyatt Regency. It's only one stop from the conference center by subway.
	Woman	Oh, great. That's perfect.
2	Man	Has anyone turned in a small black leather address book?
	Woman	Do you have any idea where you might have left it?
	Man	I'm not sure exactly, but I think it must have been at the telephone booth, next to the newsstand.
3	Man	The basic charge is $475 for one week.
	Woman	Does that include unlimited mileage?
	Man	Yes. But full insurance coverage is on top of that.

Listening 3

1 Do you offer a shuttle service from the airport?
   A Yes, 24-hour room service is available.
   B We can arrange that for a small fee.

2 If one of our guests wanted to play golf, would you be able to arrange that for us?
   A Yes, they want to.
   B We could do that.

3 In the case of a cancellation, would you return our deposit?
   A As long as you notify us at least 48 hours in advance.
   B I'm sorry. No briefcases have been turned in.

4 What can we offer our clients if they're interested in eco-tourist activities?
   A We're very interested.
   B They can choose from a range of exciting options.

Review Test 3 Units 7–9

Part 1

1 A The people are sitting indoors.
   B Dinner is being served by the pool.
   C The waiter is taking their orders.
   D The tables are set up on the sidewalk.

2 A The teller's counting out the money.
   B The woman is closing the window.
   C The customer's using an automatic teller machine.
   D She's clearing the counter.

3 A He's dropped the racket.
   B He's returning the ball.
   C He's repairing the net.
   D He's waiting for a court.

4 A The passengers are boarding the plane.
   B They're packing their bags.
   C The tourists are looking at the display.
   D They're standing in the baggage claim area.

Part 2

5 How much is the one-way fare?
   A You can pay by credit card.
   B It's very far.
   C That depends when you travel.

6 Can you tell me how long it will take to transfer the funds to my account?
   A Yes. I've taken that into account.
   B You should be credited within the next three days.
   C It only takes fifteen minutes by subway.

7 Have you paid off your mortgage yet?
   A Yes, I know. I really should pay them more.
   B No. I still have six more months to go.
   C Our hard work has really paid off.

8 Could you put that on my bill, please?
   A Certainly. If you'd just sign the check.
   B Actually, I built it myself.
   C I'm sorry but Bill is not on duty today.

9 Are you going running this afternoon or would you rather play tennis?
   A I'd prefer not to arrive too late.
   B Unfortunately, we've run into a few problems with the new tenant.
   C Sounds like fun. I'll meet you down at the court, say, around three.

10 Would you like a window or an aisle seat?
   A I'll get one for both of us.
   B A table for four, please.
   C Either is fine with me.

11 Isn't the art center open on Mondays?
   A It usually is, but they're setting up a special exhibition this week.
   B Yes, the registration fee covers all art supplies.
   C No, I sent her the artwork on Tuesday.

12 The tour guide was outstanding, don't you think?
   A Her comments were both entertaining and informative.
   B Yes. The guidelines seem to be very complete.
   C Well, I think the next tour starts in an hour.

13 Would you happen to know when the next ferry sails to the mainland?
   A It happened when they were sailing.
   B Our entire stock goes on sale tomorrow.
   C It's boarding right now from Dock 5.

Part 3
Questions 14–16:

Woman	Does the hotel offer a courtesy shuttle from the airport?
Man	Yes, we do. Pick-up is from Arrivals at Terminal 1.
Woman	Could you reserve us three places? Our flight gets in at 2 p.m.
Man	There's no need for that. There's plenty of room on board, and our service runs every 20 minutes.

Questions 17–19:

Woman	I'd like to pay for these items by credit card.
Man	I'm afraid I can't accept credit cards today because our machine isn't working. Can you pay by cash or check?
Woman	I don't have my checkbook with me, but I can go to the nearest ATM and take out some money.
Man	There's one right across the street, next to the library. I'll keep your things here at the register until you return.

Part 4
Questions 20–22:

Flight 517 to Houston will now begin boarding from gate three. As we will be boarding from the rear of the aircraft, we ask passengers sitting in rows 44 to 32 to report to gate three immediately. Please have your boarding passes ready to present to airline personnel. Passengers are reminded that federal regulations currently limit air travelers to one carry-on item per passenger.

Questions 23–25:

Welcome to the Museum of Modern Art and thank you for choosing our audio guide to accompany you on your visit. The audio guide provides commentaries about some of the paintings in our permanent collection. Before you start your visit please listen carefully to the following instructions.

Beside selected paintings, there is a white sticker with a corresponding audio guide number. To hear a commentary, enter the number displayed next to the painting. If you wish to interrupt the recording, you can press the red pause button. To restart, push the green play button. Use the arrow keys to set the volume.

Should you have any questions about the audio guide or if you experience difficulties using it, please ask the staff to help you.

Before leaving the gallery, please remember to return your audio guide to our staff. We hope that you will enjoy the museum collections.

10 Environment
Snapshot

B
A Palm trees grow along the coast.
B The cottage overlooks the sea.
C The freeway runs past the skyscrapers.
D The high-rise buildings are on opposite sides of the river.
E Cattle are grazing in a field next to the refinery.
F The farmland is being plowed for planting.
G The laundry is hanging from the balcony.
H The houses are only three stories high.

Listening 1

C
Welcome to the European weather forecast for Friday September 7th. Well, there's certainly been a lot of wet weather around for most of northern Europe over the last few days and that looks set to continue over the weekend. We have an area of low pressure moving across from southern England into continental Europe and that's bringing some very heavy rain indeed. So, much of Germany and France can expect prolonged rain during today and tomorrow which will be falling as light snow at higher altitudes as it moves through to

the Swiss Alps. Temperatures quite mild but slightly below the seasonal average; around 46 degrees in London but definitely a little warmer in Brussels with 50 degrees. That weather front is also bringing strong winds with it and the weather office has issued a storm warning for western Austria where winds are expected to be gusting at over 120 kilometers per hour. A very different picture in southern Europe where high pressure over central Spain and Portugal is creating some unusually warm weather for this time of year. Bright sunshine over most of the Mediterranean with temperatures well up in the seventies in Lisbon and an expected high of 75 degrees in Barcelona later today. Moving further east to Turkey. Mostly overcast in this part of the continent but there is a risk of some thunderstorms around the Black Sea coast.

Listening 2

1	Man	I've just been looking at the figures that the mayor announced for the new city budget.
	Woman	I heard the interview he gave on the radio. I can't believe that he's going to cut the mass transit budget again.
	Man	Me neither. He's really asking for trouble by doing that. I wouldn't be surprised if the bus drivers decide to go on strike.
2	Woman	Would you be interested in joining our car pool?
	Man	Why not? Sounds like a good idea. How does it work?
	Woman	Well, we each take turns driving. So you'd only have to use your car once a week.
3	Man	Are you going to be home this weekend?
	Woman	No actually, we're planning to go hiking, up in the mountains.
	Man	Well, make sure you take some warm clothing. The weather report said there will be frost on Saturday.
	Woman	Don't worry. We've got everything we need.
4	Woman	I'm calling about the appointment that we made for you to visit the three-bedroom apartment on Central Avenue.
	Man	That's tomorrow at ten, right?
	Woman	Well, I'm very sorry but I'm afraid we'll have to switch that to another date. The owner has just told me he won't be available then.

Listening 3

B

A   Well, there should be about 100,000 on board at any one time but only 40,000 of them will actually be residents. There will also be a crew of 20,000 and the rest will be visitors.

B   The construction phase hasn't actually started yet. But some specialists are suggesting that it could be launched within three years.

C   Well there's really no limit on where it can go. So probably it will travel regularly around the world, calling at many of the major cities with seaports.

D   It'll have a fully operational airport on the top deck – so planes will be able to fly in and out rather like on an aircraft carrier. And there will also be a marina so that smaller ships can dock with it.

E   Well, it's been designed as a city not just as a ship. So you'll have a full range of commercial activities going on inside with trade centers and so on – just like in any normal city. And, of course, you'll have schools for the children who are living on board and a fully-equipped hospital.

F   Well, there's a whole selection of real estate investment opportunities. These range from luxury suites to much more simple "living units". The starting price should be about 180,000 dollars and the top price will probably be around 40 million dollars.

G   It's a project that's attracting a lot of interest from potential residents, and that group includes not only people who are looking for a secure environment for their retirement but also business people who are interested in living and working in a city that's not part of any one nation.

H   I think that convenience is certainly one of the main factors. The idea is that this will be like a compact city and you'll have everything you need within easy reach. So there will be no need to take public transportation and, of course, the weather is another factor. The ship will be able to position itself in warm weather all year round – and that's certainly a major advantage.

11 Health

Snapshot

B

A   They're exercising on the beach.

B   He's kneeling next to the patient.

C   They're lifting weights in the gym.

D   The physical therapist is stretching the patient's arm.

E   They're balancing on one leg.

F   The doctor's examining the man's chest.

G   They're holding hands.

H   The relief workers are handing out food.

Listening 1

B

1	Man 1	So you're in for your annual check-up and cleaning, is that it?
	Man 2	Yes. And I was wondering if you could take a look at one of my molars on the top left. It's been sore lately, especially when I chew.
	Man 1	OK, I'll have a look and then take an X-ray. Open wide, please.

2	Woman	Do you remember when you last came in for a complete physical?
	Man	Actually, it was some time ago. Four, maybe, five years.
	Woman	You know, even if you're in good health, you should see a doctor every two years for a check-up.
	Man	You're right. But I never seem to have enough time.
3	Man	Hi. I'd like to have this prescription filled, please.
	Woman	Certainly. Which would you prefer: brand name medicine or the less expensive generic drugs?
	Man	Hmm. I think I'll go with the brand name, since that's what my doctor's prescribed.
4	Man 1	Will I have to wear corrective lenses all the time?
	Man 2	No, no. You have very good eyesight. This prescription will correct your vision so that you can read comfortably at night.
	Man 1	That's good news.
5	Woman 1	The health insurance benefits package we offer our employees includes full medical and dental coverage.
	Woman 2	Will my policy include prescription drugs?
	Woman 1	Yes, it does. It reimburses 90% of all doctor-prescribed medications.

Listening 2

Now for those of you who may be thinking that it's high time to switch to a new healthier diet, we've got just the thing. On May 15th the United Okinawa Association is organizing a special evening event where you'll have the opportunity to meet two of the authors of the best-selling *Okinawa Diet Plan*. Doctors Craig and Bradley Willcox will be giving a short presentation of their research on the Okinawa community and explaining what makes it so unique. Don't forget, that's May 15th from six to nine at the community center in Waikiki. Seating is limited so you'd better book early. Tickets to the event are on sale for 40 dollars and that includes the price of your personal hardcover copy of the book that could help you to get leaner, live longer and never feel hungry. Sample Okinawan recipes will be available for tasting after the presentation. For further information about the event and to make a telephone reservation, call 215-658-4321.

Listening 3

A	Woman	How about targeting schools?
	Man	Excellent idea. We can be sure that every child in school would have the opportunity to be vaccinated.

B	Man	We should provide mayors with information that will help them support vaccination programs for their communities.
	Woman	I agree. And how about developing neighborhood vaccination workshops to involve people on a local level?
C	Man	We ought to approach companies that market children's products.
	Woman	That's not a bad idea. Why not approach the President's wife, too? She's a great supporter of public health issues.
D	Man 1	How should we evaluate the success of the Vaccination Week campaign?
	Man 2	Why don't we conduct a public awareness survey afterward?
E	Woman 1	What about posters? They're inexpensive and can be widely distributed.
	Woman 2	Great idea. Couldn't we also get national television stations to donate air time for our commercials?

12 Society

Snapshot

B

A The schoolchildren are clapping their hands.
B The law enforcement officers are on patrol.
C The candidate is making a speech.
D The people are registering to vote.
E The court session is held outside.
F The police are writing out a traffic ticket.
G The lawyers are meeting in the court house.
H The woman is filling out a form.
I The instructor is calling on the students.
J The court officials are facing the people.
K The policemen are riding bicycles.
L Some students are raising their hands.

Listening 1

C

1	Woman	Do you have a currently valid form of photo ID, your birth certificate, and proof of residence?
	Man	Yes, I do. By the way, if I register today, will I be eligible to vote in the upcoming elections?
	Woman	Yes. You'll receive your official voter registration card indicating your local polling place in the mail within a few days.
2	Man 1	Good morning, sir. May I see your driver's license and vehicle registration, please?
	Man 2	Certainly, here you are. Is there something wrong, officer? Was I speeding?

Man 1	Not to worry, sir. We pulled you over because we noticed that your left brake light is out. You'll need to get that fixed as soon as possible.
3 Woman 1	What a weekend! I spent the whole time filling out my income tax returns.
Woman 2	Oh, that's right! I totally forgot. When are they due again?
Woman 1	You have until midnight Wednesday to file. Hope yours are less complicated than mine!
4 Man	If elected, what will be your top priority during your first six months in office?
Woman	If I become mayor of this city, I will devote time and effort to improving the local school system. We need to develop our educational facilities.
Man	Does that mean that you would raise local taxes?
Woman	Oh. I think we could find other ways of financing that.
5 Man	Have you seen the continuing education course catalog for next semester?
Woman	I think I saw one in the HR office yesterday. Were you considering taking some classes?
Man	Yes. In fact, I'm only six credits away from completing my MBA in the university's professional business progam.

Listening 2

C

I would like to thank you for showing interest in our Legal Aid Volunteer Program here on the Hopi reservation. As you know the Hopi tribal council is looking for lawyers to volunteer their time to provide legal advice to Hopi tribal members. This is important because although Native American Reservations are within the borders of the United States, the tribes have independent governments whose legal policies and practices differ from state and federal law. For example, did you know that within the Hopi reservation, laws are enforced, not by federal, state, or county police, but by Hopi Tribal Rangers? This three-day seminar will introduce you to the basic governmental and legal differences between Hopi culture and the surrounding United States. This knowledge will enable you to better inform tribal members of their legal rights regarding such important issues as reclaiming lands belonging to the tribe, securing the right to manage the natural resources within tribal property and, more generally, expanding Native American autonomy in order to preserve Hopi language, culture and traditions.

Listening 3

B

1 What's your position on this issue?
  A We're standing near the exit.
  B By and large, I share the same opinion as Sally.

2 Could you expand on that, please?
  A I'd be glad to go into greater depth.
  B Yes. Let's move to a larger room.

3 Wouldn't you agree that video games are completely harmless?
  A Well, I wouldn't go that far.
  B Yes. We greeted them at the door.

4 Do you realize that companies would lose subscribers?
  A Yes. We'd really like to come.
  B That won't necessarily happen.

Review Test 4 Units 10–12

Part 1

1 A The patient is wearing a watch.
  B She's reading the manual.
  C He's looking for his glasses.
  D She's checking the patient's eyes.

2 A He's clearing the snow away.
  B He's showing his house.
  C The street is covered with snow.
  D He's shoveling the soil in his garden.

3 A The parking lot is full.
  B There's an overpass across the freeway.
  C Traffic is stopped in both directions.
  D The commuters are riding the bus.

4 A The man is waving to the cyclists.
  B He's raising his arm above his head.
  C The man is directing traffic.
  D He's pointing out the problem.

Part 2

5 Where do you stand on this issue?
  A Yes, we're near the elevator.
  B Over there, next to the photocopier.
  C I share Don's point of view.

6 How about next Tuesday for your annual check-up?
  A It's about the checking account.
  B That would be fine.
  C About twice a week.

7 Wouldn't it be better to get a second opinion?
  A You're right. It wouldn't help at all.
  B Good idea. Let's ask Toshiro.
  C Unfortunately, the results haven't improved.

8 May I have this prescription filled, please?
  A I'm sorry. There's no more room.
  B I'll need to order this. You can pick it up this afternoon.
  C It certainly is very filling.

9 Have you heard the weather report?
  A Yes, the announcement was delayed.
  B I'm not sure whether it's hers.
  C The forecast is for clear, sunny skies.

10 Would you be interested in joining our fitness group?
  A Thank you for asking, but I already have a membership at the gym.
  B Could you get me a larger size? This one doesn't fit.
  C Yes, we can open a joint account.

11 When do we need to submit our planning application?
  A To the planning department.
  B Next Tuesday at the latest.
  C By two members of the department.

12 Didn't you think that last apartment was too small?
  A But considering the location it's a great deal.
  B We were thinking about going to the mall.
  C Yes, it lasted longer than I thought it would.

13 When will the commuter lanes re-open?
  A We'd be more than happy to pass on the message.
  B Not before next week. Until then we'll just have to leave earlier.
  C You can come as late as you want.

14 Did the doctor tell you to change your diet?
  A He didn't say anything about that.
  B Yes. I'm meeting them at four.
  C No, I can't tell the difference.

Part 3

Questions 15–17:

Man	John said that you are moving into a new house in the suburbs. Is that right?
Woman	Yes. Real-estate prices were so high that we couldn't afford to buy in the city.
Man	I know what you mean. Housing costs have skyrocketed in the last year.
Woman	Yeah. We were lucky to get it for such a good price.

Questions 18–20:

Man	Hi, Mary. You're in early this morning, aren't you? I thought you usually started at nine.
Woman	Well, I used to, yes. But I've decided to start work one hour earlier every day. That way I don't get stuck in traffic on my way in and when I go home.
Man	I wish I could do the same, but there's no way I can start this early every day. I usually have to drop the kids at school before I get here.
Woman	Well, you'd certainly save some time if you could. I reckon it's reduced my travel time by at least an hour every day.

Part 4

Questions 21–23:

Hi, my name's Steve Zachery and I'll be leading today's seminar entitled "On-the-job Fitness". We will be looking at how and why your company should consider developing a corporate fitness program. But let's begin with the bottom line; what are the real, tangible benefits of a corporate fitness program? Human resources directors that have implemented complete health plans have reported many positive outcomes. These benefits range from fewer worker absences to better attitudes, greater corporate loyalty, and less stress. Companies have also found such fitness programs to be a valuable recruiting tool that improves employee retention. One of the most significant long-term advantages is reduced health insurance costs for you and your employees. These are just a few of the points we'll be covering today in greater detail. So turning to ...

Questions 24–26:

The National Weather Service has issued a winter weather advisory for tonight. Temperatures over the state will remain cold enough to produce steady snow through at least midnight. Snow is expected to accumulate from three to five inches across Jefferson County, while four to six inches are likely in Madison County. Motorists are urged to exercise caution while driving. Many roads across the advisory area will be snow-covered and icy. Due to the heavy amounts of snow, schools in Jefferson and Madison Counties have announced a "Delayed opening" tomorrow. School will begin one hour later than normal in order to allow road crews to clear roads and highways. In the event that heavy snow makes it dangerous to hold regular classes and forces closure of school, an announcement will be made by the school district and broadcast tomorrow morning at 6 a.m. on this and other radio stations. Stay tuned for further information.

Suggestions for additional Speaking and Writing practice

A suggested list of extra speaking and writing activities is given below. All of the activities listed here will help you to prepare for tasks that are featured on the TOEIC® Speaking and Writing Tests. For a full description of the Speaking and Writing tests see the Teacher's Book or consult the TOEIC® website at www.ets.org/toeic or www.toeic.com.

Speaking Practice

Reading Aloud

Practice reading aloud short texts and short extracts from articles (approx. 70–100 words). You can also select extracts from the audioscripts at the back of the book, record yourself and then compare your readings with the recordings on the CDs.

Describing a Picture

Practice making short descriptions of pictures. You can use pictures from either the coursebook units or the review tests. Limit your descriptions to 30 seconds of speaking time. Make several statements about each picture and give a general description of the scene that it shows. You can include references to your own experience and knowledge.

Responding to Questions

Practice responding to questions. Use the questions on page 14 and give short responses. Record yourself and compare your responses with the recordings on the CDs.

Expressing an Opinion

Use the questions and discussion topics in the coursebook and practice giving one-minute spoken presentations of your opinions. You can find examples of appropriate questions and topics on pages 9, 13, 17, 23, 52, 70, 86, 90, 100, 102 and 105.

Writing Practice

Writing Sentences about Pictures

Choose some of your own pictures and write one statement about each. Bring your selection of pictures to class. Select two of the words that you have used to describe each picture (for example a verb and a preposition) and put them on a slip of paper or Post-it note. Exchange your pictures and notes with another student. You should each write one sentence about each picture using the words on the notes.

Writing Emails

Practice writing email responses to problems and enquiries. You can use the situations that are presented in the communication activities to give you the scenario for your emails. Write a short email to one of the people involved in the activities that are presented on pages 24, 32, 54, 62, 76, 92, 106 and 114.

Write Short Essays

Use the discussion topics or questions that follow or precede the Viewpoint articles to prepare one or more short essays. You should express your opinion about the topic, explain your reasons and include examples. Limit the length of your essay to 300 words. You can find examples of appropriate questions and topics on pages 13, 23, 52, 90, 102 and 105.

Answer Key

Unit 1 Careers

Snapshot

1 c   2 b   3 b   4 a

Listening 1

A 1 availability, contract(s), a previous assignment
2 availability, contract(s), an assignment abroad, meeting arrangements
3 contract(s), a replacement

B **Call 1**
Name of caller Jason Jackman
Subject of call Asking if Sabrina Marquez can do another contract
Action to be taken Laura to check on January contract and get back to Jason tomorrow

Call 2
Name of caller Howard Mason
Subject of call Wants to hire two truck drivers to deliver merchandise to Mexico
Action to be taken Laura to go for meeting at Howard's office tomorrow at 11 a.m. to go over the conditions and contract

Call 3
Name of caller Laura Alvarado
Subject of call Chef currently on temporary assignment has resigned to take up full-time post without giving notice
Action to be taken New chef to call Manfred first thing tomorrow

Grammar Check 1

A 1 c   2 a   3 b   4 d
B 1 b   2 d   3 a   4 c

C 1 is releasing
2 is changing
3 examines
4 compares
5 show
6 appears
7 expect
8 agrees
9 possesses
10 are becoming
11 suggest
12 do not have

Vocabulary Builder

A 1 Paul Gauguin, painter – stockbroker
2 Charles Lindbergh, aviator – farmer
3 Alfred Hitchcock, film director – clerk
4 Marilyn Monroe, actress – factory worker
5 Ralph Lauren, fashion designer – salesman
6 J K Rowling, author – secretary
7 Hillary Clinton, senator – lawyer

B 1 -ist: publicist, biologist, pharmacist, receptionist, economist
2 -ian: optician, electrician, statistician, historian, librarian
3 -er: laborer, designer, engineer
 -or: supervisor, surveyor
4 -ee: trainee, referee, trustee, addressee, interviewee
5 -ant: consultant, accountant, attendant, assistant
 -ent: correspondent
6 -man / -woman: fireman, salesman, saleswoman, repairman, craftsman, craftswoman, chairman, chairwoman

C 1 consultants / accountants
2 chairman / chairwoman
3 electrician
4 economists

Viewpoint

1 To learn global-employee skills.
2 How to interact with people from other cultures.
3 You should not slap him / her on the back or call him/her by his / her first name in the first meeting.
4 They have improved the image of Indian companies and allowed them to work on bigger projects at better rates.

Grammar Check 2

A 1 c   2 a   3 b
 4 e   5 d   6 f
B 1 Where
2 When
3 How many
4 What / How many
5 Who
6 How much / What
7 Which / What / How many
8 How

"What / How many languages are you fluent in?" is the only legal question.

Listening 2

1 A   2 F   3 E
4 G   5 C

There are no responses for questions B and D.

Listening 3

A 1 recruiters, headhunters
2 job-seekers, job-hunters
3 interviewing, e-recruiting

B Don Stanley
1 15-minute interview
2 shorter, not longer
3 hiring professionals, not interviewees

Kimberly Armstrong
1 job interviews, not advertisements
2 job-seekers, not interviewers
3 job-seekers, not recruiters

Unit 2 Workplaces

Snapshot

A 1 **Laboratory**

Objects lab equipment, bottles, containers, pippet, test tubes, jars, solutions.

Job laboratory technician

2 **Architect's office**

Objects drawing, ruler, drawing board, model.

Job architect

3 **Garage workshop**

Objects car, tools, battery, engine, hood, fender, wheel, tire.

Job mechanic

4 **Warehouse**

Objects forklift, stock, coils, pallets.

Job warehouse worker, forklift driver.

B (suggested answers)

1 The man is filling some containers.

The work surface is covered with equipment.

The wall cabinets are used for storage.

He's carrying out a test.

The staff are wearing lab coats.

2 The woman is working on a plan.

There is a model on the table.

She's drawing a line on the plan.

The blinds are drawn.

There is a table behind the woman.

3 He's repairing the engine of a car.

The hood of the car is open.

The man is fixing the car.

The battery is on the floor.

4 The workman is moving some goods with a forklift.

The warehouse is stocked with goods.

The coils are stacked on top of each other.

He's moving the goods from one place to another.

Grammar Check 1

A 1 a   2 b   3 b
   4 a   5 b

B 1 result
2 architecture
3 furniture
4 Researchers
5 work
6 impact
7 privacy
8 teams
9 transition
10 people

Listening 1

B   1 J   2 A   3 H   4 F   5 D
    6 B   7 G   8 I   9 E   10 C

Grammar Check 2

A 1 around
2 opposite
3 along
4 alongside
5 under
6 through
7 toward(s)
8 within
9 above
10 against

B inside   8
beneath   5
with   6
beside   4
down   3
to   7
round   1
across from   2
over   9

C 1 d
2 c
3 d
4 a
5 d
6 b

Listening 2

A 1 **paperwork**
faxes, envelopes, <u>documents</u>, letters
2 **publications**
directories, magazines, <u>books</u>, <u>manuals</u>
3 **office supplies**
stapler, scissors, pens, paper clips
4 **electrical equipment**
<u>computer</u>, lamp, <u>fan</u>, <u>mouse</u>, <u>keyboard</u>, <u>headphones</u>
5 **personal items**
photos, <u>certificate</u>, <u>knick-knacks</u>, <u>mug</u>, <u>poster</u>, bag

B See objects underlined in **A**.

C 1 invoices   in-box tray
2 price lists   shelf on the left
3 personal items   shelf on the right
4 customer files   filing cabinet, computer
5 printer cartridges   filing cabinet drawer

Active Practice

(suggested answers)
Student A
The pencils are beside the notebook.
The cup is on the desk.
The picture is on the wall on the right of the filing cabinet.
Student B
One pencil is on the notebook.
One pencil is on the right of the mouse pad.
The cup is on the filing cabinet.
The picture is on the wall on the left of the filing cabinet.
Other objects in different places are:
the plants, the eraser, the notebook, the trashcan, the mouse, the biscuit, the filing cabinet.

Vocabulary Builder

A 1 reform, uniform
2 conform, deform, inform, perform, reform, transform
3 former, formative, formal
4 formalist, formality
5 formally, formerly
6 formation

B 7 conformist, conformity, deformation, deformity, informal, informant, information, informer informality, performance, performer, reformation, reformer, transformation, transformer.

C 1 former
2 formal
3 uniforms
4 forms
5 performance

Viewpoint

B 1 a   2 a   3 c

Listening 3

A 1 request
2 issue
3 assign
4 review
5 suggest
6 express
7 discuss

B A issue instructions
B discuss problems
C express opinions

Unit 3
Communications
Snapshot

A (possible statements)

1 She's reading a newspaper.
She's at a newsstand.
There are many newspapers displayed on the rack.

2 She's talking on the phone.
She's calling from a public phone.
She's using a payphone.

3 She's mailing letters / packages.
She's dropping the mail into the box.
The mailbox is on the sidewalk.

4 She's working on a computer.
She's looking at the screen.
She's reading / checking her email.

B 1 D, G
2 E, H
3 A, C
4 B, F

Vocabulary Builder

A and B
Broadcasting
cable television
news bulletin
Press
feature article
front page
Information Technology
web browser
computer screen
Telecommunications
voice mail
phone booth
Postal Services
mailbox
post office

C 1 voice mail
2 feature article, front page
3 mailbox, post office

D (suggested answers)

press
press agency
press agent
press book
press bureau
press campaign
press pass
press photographer
press release

phone
phone call
phone bill
phone book
phone booth
phone message
phone number
cell phone
portable phone

news
news agency
newsagent*
newscaster
newsletter*
newspaper*
newsprint*
news rack
newsroom*
newsstand*
(*some compound nouns become combined into single words)

Listening 1

A 1 customer & news agent: at a newsstand, buying Italian newspapers

2 traveler & airport employee: at an airport, finding a courtesy phone / a lost suitcase

3 co-workers: in an office, sending a contract by fax or by mail

4 colleagues or friends: in front of a TV, watching the news

5 computer user & computer technician: in front of a computer, typing in the email log-in and password

B (suggested answers)

1 newspapers, sell out, magazines

2 name being paged, courtesy phone, baggage claim, found, suitcase

3 mail, contract, fax, to send, mail pick-up

4 to watch, evening news, station, channel, coverage

5 type in, log-in, password, check email, computer

Grammar Check 1

A 1 a, an, the
2 the
3 a / an
4 the
5 television, because it's a general noun

B 1 The
2 the or no article
3 a
4 the
5 an or the
6 the
7 the
8 a
9 no article
10 no article
11 a
12 the
13 no article
14 the

Viewpoint

1 talking on a cell phone, sending text messages, email, bulletin-board postings, chat lines
2 They're considered to be more reliable.
3 A company sent text messages to employees to lay them off.

Discussion

1 faxes, office memos, surface mail, telegrams, flyers, billboards, posters

Listening 2

A caller: 3, 5, 7, 9, 10
receiver: 1, 2, 4, 6, 8

B
1 A	2 H	3 B
4 I	5 E	6 J
7 C	8 G	9 D
10 F		

Grammar Check 2

A 1 past simple
present perfect
2 past simple
present perfect
present perfect

B 1 have had
2 opened
3 has moved
4 relocated
5 updated
6 have slowed
7 changed
8 did you switch
9 didn't
10 upgraded

Listening 3

1 hold a press conference
2 laid off 1,000 workers
3 prospects are not good
4 moved operations to cheaper labor markets

Review Test 1
Units 1–3

Listening Test

PART 1

1 D	2 A	3 C
4 D		

PART 2

5 C	6 A	7 B
8 B	9 A	10 B
11 C	12 A	13 B

PART 3

14 A	15 B	16 C
17 C	18 B	19 B

PART 4

20 C	21 A	22 B
23 C	24 D	25 C

Reading Test

PART 5

26 D	27 A	28 B
29 B	30 A	31 B
32 D	33 C	34 B
35 C	36 C	37 C

PART 6

38 D	39 D	40 C
41 B		

PART 7

42 D	43 C	44 A
45 C	46 D	47 D
48 C	49 B	50 B

Unit 4 Retailing

Snapshot

A (suggested answers)

1 The woman is doing her shopping at the market.
The woman is putting the fruit into a bag.
2 The customer is paying for the goods.
The saleswoman is handing the woman her change.
3 The saleswoman is explaining how to operate the television.
They're buying a television.
4 The sales clerk is arranging the items on display.
She's cleaning the counter.

B 1 A
2 C
3 H
4 F

C (suggested synonyms)

purchase – buy
give a refund – reimburse
hand – give
open – use
set up – install
arrange – place
return – bring back
explain – demonstrate

Listening 1

A and B

1	briefcase	leather goods
2	notecards	stationery
3	chest of drawers	home furnishings
4	espresso machine	electrical appliances
5	gold bracelet	jewelry
6	jigsaw puzzle	toys and games
7	MP3 player	TV / Hi-Fi
8	perfume	cosmetics
9	shawl	women's fashion
10	tablecloth	household linens

C Location and request

1 teenage fashion
help with choice of gift
2 welcome and info desk / customer services
information about a special delivery service
3 toys / games
information about a product

Grammar Check 1

A

1 a Comparatives: add -er;
Superlatives: add -est
b Change the final y to i and then add the same endings as for one- or two-syllable adjectives
c Comparatives: more/less before the adjective; Superlatives: the most / the least before the adjective

2 a as + adjective + as
b comparative adjective + than

3 a no
b yes

B 1 Our repairmen are the *loneliest* guys in town.
2 Correct.
3 The *most* refreshing drink in the world.
4 If only everything in life was as reliable *as* a Volkswagen.
5 No battery is *stronger* for longer.
6 The world's *most* trusted anti-virus solution.
7 *The* best a man can get.
8 If you find it *cheaper*, we pay you the difference.
9 Correct.

Viewpoint

A 1 text A
2 texts B / C
3 text B
4 text B
5 text D
6 texts B / C

B 1 Madrid, London, Tokyo
2 Barcelona
3 more than one thousand
4 customers sit on steps
5 the cuisine is natural – food is prepared in front of customers, bioconstruction
6 images, icons, objects, shoes
7 boxing glove
8 no left or right shoe

Listening 2

New sector of activity: hotels
Location: Barcelona
Unique features: two spaces in each room (bedroom and lounge area), Internet Wi-Fi and plasma-screen TV, hammock, 24-hour access to free buffet
Customer feedback: very positive, would like more Camper hotels
Future plans: build a second hotel in Mallorca

Vocabulary Builder

A 1 over   2 re   3 bi
4 inter   5 under   6 up
7 sub   8 co   9 un
10 mis   11 out   12 dis

B 1 up   2 over/under
3 mis   4 dis
5 re   6 sub

C 1 disabled
2 overcharged / undercharged
3 renegotiate
4 discontinued
5 mismanagement
6 underestimate
7 oversize

Grammar Check 2

A affirmative
negative

B 1 is there
2 doesn't it
3 are they
4 do I
5 will it
6 won't it
7 didn't you
8 could you

Listening 3

1 D   2 G   3 F
4 A   5 E   6 B
7 H   8 C

Unit 5 Industry

Snapshot

A (suggested answers)

1 Shoes are being manufactured on an assembly line. The line workers are using special machines and are wearing short-sleeved blouses and bonnets.
2 An inspector is checking a tank at a refinery where gas is being produced. He is wearing a hard hat and black overalls.
3 A team of carpenters is building a structure out of wood. They are wearing hard hats and have tool belts.
4 A steelworker is pouring molten steel. He's wearing gloves and goggles (protective eyewear).

B 1 B, E   2 A, D   3 F, H
4 C, G

Grammar Check 1

A 1 The raw materials are being mixed in large basins.

2 The workers are mixing the raw materials in large basins.

B *to be*, past

C are blended
are added
is cooked
are dropped
are transferred

D 1 sent
2 sugarcoated
3 given
4 heaped
5 called
6 added

E 7 are poured
8 is sifted
9 is polished
10 are seasoned
11 is inserted
12 is printed
13 are packaged, have been packaged
14 are loaded
15 (are) transported

Listening 1

1 C   2 D   3 B
4 A   5 E

Vocabulary Builder

A 1 mended ✓ repaired ✓ damaged ✗
2 maintained ✓ neglected ✗ serviced ✓
3 modernized ✓ outdated ✗ renovated ✓
4 stored ✗ gotten rid of ✓ thrown away ✓

B 1 fixed
2 looked after
3 refurbished
4 discarded

C 1 modernized / renovated / refurbished
2 neglected / damaged
3 thrown away / gotten rid of / discarded
4 fixed / mended / repaired

D 1 outmoded
2 cared for
3 kept
4 broken

Listening 2

A 1 - 2 B 3 D
4 E 5 - 6 C
7 A

B 1 C 2 D 3 E
4 A 5 B 6 -
7 -

C 1 ~~wearing~~ worn
2 ~~conduct~~ conducted
3 ~~been~~ be
4 ~~is~~ are
5 ~~keeping~~ kept
6 ~~from~~ by
7 ~~ask~~ asked

Viewpoint

1 D 2 B

Grammar Check 2

A 1 got / forced / allowed (type 2)
had / made / let (type 1)
had / got (type 3)
2 have = get
make = force
let = allow
3 ask, convince, encourage

B 1 re-install
2 approved
3 inspect
4 by
5 take
6 to increase
7 have
8 to transfer

Listening 3

1 an industrial park
2 domestic items, finely worked gold jewelry, small statues
3 construction workers
4 local Chamber of Commerce

Unit 6 Trade

Snapshot

A 1 a worker is arranging fruit
2 an auctioneer is managing an auction
3 a dockworker is signaling as a container is being moved
4 traders are working at an international exchange

B 1 wholesale food market, fruit and produce
2 auction house, artwork
3 cargo containers, international port
4 financial market, stocks and commodities

D 1 D, H 2 C, F 3 A, G
4 B, E

Listening 1

A 1 shipping
2 packing
3 bidding and purchasing
4 clearing customs and paying duties and tariffs
5 insuring

B 1 send, sculptures, by air, ocean freight, transit, arrive in time, art fair
2 packing list, container, to inventory, breakable, vases, designated
3 drawing, museum, collection, the reserve price, acquisitions budget, bidding
4 paintings, re-export, duty fees, departure
5 policy, cover, shipment

Grammar Check 1

A future actions and predictions: 3, *will* + verb
future plans or intentions: 4, *going to* + verb
future arrangements: 1, *be* + *-ing* (present continuous)
schedules: 2, present simple

B 1 handle
2 will make
3 are
4 begins
5 is going
6 receive
7 is going
8 arrives

Listening 2

1 $3.75
2 labor at shop
3 $1.29
4 shop owner's profit
5 $0.47
6 farmer's and grower's share

Viewpoint

B 1 early next year
2 $8.4 billion
3 specialty coffee shops
4 $0.04–0.05
5 roads, schools, health centers, housing

Grammar Check 2

A a 3 b 5 c 1
d 2 / 4 e 2 / 4

B 1 reasons
2 led to / resulted in
3 result
4 effects
5 Since / As

Listening 3

A 1 minutes
2 agenda
3 item
4 views
5 break
6 business
7 chair

B 1 chair
2 business
3 break
4 agenda
5 item
6 views
7 minutes

C 1 B 2 A 3 A
4 B 5 B 6 A
7 B

Vocabulary Builder

A 1 e 2 f 3 a
4 b 5 d 6 c

B 1 beside the point
2 point out
3 point of view
4 pointless
5 to the point
6 makes a point

Communication

A 1 to support producers and reduce poverty in developing countries
2 by promoting sales of Fairtrade products

Review Test 2
Units 4–6
Listening Test

PART 1

1 C	2 D	3 D
4 A		

PART 2

5 A	6 B	7 C
8 B	9 B	10 A
11 B	12 C	13 B

PART 3

14 B	15 D	16 B
17 D	18 B	19 A

PART 4

20 A	21 B	22 B
23 B	24 C	25 B

Reading Test

PART 5

26 C	27 C	28 B
29 D	30 C	31 D
32 A	33 C	34 B
35 C	36 B	37 A

PART 6

38 B	39 A	40 D
41 A		

PART 7

42 C	43 D	44 B
45 A	46 C	47 B
48 D	49 C	50 D

Unit 7 Leisure
Snapshot

A (suggested answers)

1 The men are in a swimming pool.
   They are playing board games /
   chess.
2 The three women are walking in
   the wilderness.
   They are backpacking.
   They are crossing a stream / river /
   creek.

3 They're playing soccer.
   The teams are on the playing field.
   The ball is above the goal.
4 The couple is eating at a
   restaurant.
   They're dining on the terrace.
   They're enjoying their meal
   outside.

B 1 F   2 E   3 G
   4 H

Listening 1

A 1 e
   2 d
   3 b
   4 g
   5 h
   6 f
   7 a
   8 c

B 1 watching television
   2 shopping
   3 eating out
   4 81%
   5 8%
   6 women
   7 biking
   8 men
   9 golf
   10 jogging

Grammar Check 1

A *who* for people
   that for things and people
   whose for possessions
   where for places

B 1 Svetlana, who won the national
      junior tournament, taught me
      how to play chess.
   2 The Olympic Games, which
      originated in Greece, are held
      every four years.
   3 My best friend, whose hobby is
      doing magic, can do the most
      amazing card tricks.

C 1 that
   2 who
   3 which
   4 where
   5 whose

Viewpoint

A (sample answers)

Texts A

1 The article presents a drive-in movie
   theater for snowmobiles. The email
   is a suggestion to submit a film to a
   festival.
2 The people who go to this movie
   theater are the Samis, who are
   Norway's indigenous people, many
   of whom are reindeer farmers.
   Lindsay is writing an email to
   Nukka.
3 In Norway.
4 The film festival takes place in the
   outdoor movie theater.

Texts B

1 The article describes a type of golf
   that is not played on traditional golf
   courses. The letter is a response to a
   request to sponsor a cross-golf
   tournament.
2 Cross-golfers; the organizer of a
   cross-golf tournament (Mr. Singh)
   and someone who works for a golf-
   equipment manufacturer (Stanley
   Baker Johnston III).
3 Cross-golf can be played anywhere
   – in cities, in hotels, along rivers.
4 The letter refuses a request to
   sponsor a cross-golf tournament.

B (sample questions)

Texts A

How do cinema-goers get to the
drive-in theater?
What is the movie theater made of?
What do the people sit on?
What is the traditional occupation
of the Samis?
What kind of movies do they show?
What does the Sami Film Festival
promote?

Texts B

What are other names for "cross-
golf"?
In what countries is cross-golf most
popular?
Who started cross-golf? Where did
he first start playing it?
In a recent tournament, what was
the "hole" that players had to hit
the golf ball into?
Why does Mr. Johnston refuse to
sponsor the tournament?

Grammar Check 2

A The order of the subject and the verb is inverted.
Direct question: verb + subject
Indirect question: subject + verb

B
1 we can find
2 you could make
3 the fish is
4 today's dessert special is

Listening 2

1 C   2 A   3 C

Vocabulary Builder

A  (tired) boring (interested) exciting
surprising (relaxed) (interested)
(relaxed) (excited)

B 1 relaxed
2 surprised
3 bored
4 tiring
5 interesting
6 exciting
7 relaxing

Listening 3

B 1 playing ping-pong: tables with nets, paddles, balls
2 going to art exhibitions: show, works, gallery, paintings, sculptures, catalog
3 watching baseball: game, inning, home run, bases, hitter, fielder, bat
4 cooking: cuisine class, dessert and pastry course, restaurant
5 playing the piano: keys, classical, improvise, jazz

Unit 8 Money

Snapshot

A (suggested answers)
1 In the front office of a bank. The bank teller is giving a customer some information. A customer is making an enquiry.

2 Beside two Automated Teller Machines.
They are taking out / withdrawing money.
They are standing next to the machine.
They are waiting to take out / withdraw money.
3 In the office of a money changer. The woman is holding up some banknotes.
She is inspecting some banknotes. The customer is leaning on the counter.
He is holding some notes in his hands.
4 At the printing office of the Federal reserve (the government department that is responsible for printing new money).
The woman is checking sheets of newly-printed dollar bills.

B and C

1D assisting = helping
2B withdrawing = taking out
3A converting = changing, exchanging
4C checking = inspecting, verifying, looking over

Listening 1

A
footwear	7/8
vehicle insurance	1/2
school tuition	9/10
mortgage	3/4
utility bills	3/4
tolls	1/2
medical coverage	5/6
groceries	7/8
allowance	9/10
club membership	11/12
prescription medicine	5/6
concert tickets	11/12

B 1 transport
2 entertainment / leisure
3 housing (renting an apartment)
4 housing (utility bills – cost of electricity)

C charge, estimate, cost, afford, rent

Grammar Check 1

A
upward	downward
1 increase	1 lower
2 raise	2 reduce
3 grow	fall
go up	go down
rise	decrease
	drop
	decline

B noun forms
increase	decrease
raise	reduction
growth	fall
rise	drop
	decline

C 1 from … to …
2 by (50%)

D Bar chart illustrates downward trend. Graph illustrates upward trend.

E 1 Reducing
2 fell / decreased / declined / went down / dropped
3 from … to
4 rise / increase / grow / go up
5 increasing
6 raise / increase
7 has grown / has increased
8 by
9 reduction
10 increase

Listening 2

A 1 the stock market   D
2 inheritance   E
3 retirement   C
4 selling a property   A
5 pay   B

B appreciate, salary, raise, pension fund, stocks, invest, inherited, investment, return

Vocabulary Builder

A 1 *broken down*   had mechanical problems
2 *carry out*   make
3 *take out*   purchase
4 *deal with*   handle
5 *go through*   discuss / explain

B 1 take out
2 took up
3 work out
4 looks after
5 bringing out
6 look up
7 bring forward
8 turned down
9 set out
10 set up

C
check	out / up
come	down / forward / out
cut	down / out / up
fall	down / out
get	down / out / up
go	after / down / forward / out / up
look	after / down / forward (to) / out / up
make	out / up
pay	out / up
put	down / forward / out / up
run	after / down / out (of) / up
settle	down / up

Viewpoint

B 1 d opened a restaurant
2 c leave the rat race
3 a salesman
4 c He left his job.

Grammar Check 2

A 1 b 2 a 3 c
4 a 5 a 6 c
7 a 8 b/c

B 1 b 2 a 3 a
4 a 5 a 6 b

Listening 3

1 Local Exchange Trading System
2 In Canada.
3 extremely successful
4 You exchange services or goods without using money.

Unit 9 Travel

Snapshot

B 1 clearing airport security
2 visiting a museum
3 taking a cab
4 checking in at an airport

C (suggested answers)
1 He's clearing airport security.
She's checking his carry-on items.
His belongings are in the bins.
2 They're visiting a museum.
They're looking at the sculptures.
They're admiring the artwork.
3 They're taking a cab.
The taxi is driving down the street.
Two people are riding in the back of a taxi.
4 They're checking in at an airport.
They're waiting at the check-in counter.

Listening 1

A 1 1 C
2 E
3 H
2 1 B, D
2 A, F
3 C, E
3 1 On a tour boat, river cruise or ferry.
2 On a train.
3 On a cruise ship, ferry, or boat.

Grammar Check 1

A have to / require / need to / don't … have to / must / must not
1 must, have to, require, need to
2 don't have to
3 must not

B 1 need / require
2 must / have to / need to
3 don't have to / need not
4 have to
5 must not
6 must / has to
7 must / have to
8 have to
9 required
10 need to / have to

Listening 2

A change money 1
register for flight 4
medical assistance 2
car rental 6
lost items 3
find a hotel 5

B 1 tourist information (5), looking for a hotel
2 lost and found (3), looking for a personal item
3 car rental (6), getting car rental information

Vocabulary Builder

A 1 careless
2 primary (primal)
3 persuasive
4 reasonable
5 original
6 familiar
7 different
8 republican
9 electronic
10 passionate
11 accessible
12 observant

B
1	careless	carelessly
2	primary	primarily
3	persuasive	persuasively
4	reasonable	reasonably
5	original	originally
6	familiar	familiarly
7	different	differently
8	republican	–
9	electronic	electronically
10	passionate	passionately
11	accessible	–
12	observant	–

C 1 prestigious
2 panoramic
3 spacious
4 complimentary
5 recreational
6 exclusively
7 professional
8 comfortably
9 knowledgeable
10 effective

Viewpoint

1 c   2 b

Grammar Check 2

A (suggested answers)

a future event that is not likely to happen 3
a future event that is likely to happen 1
a general state that is always true 2
verb tenses
1 present simple, future (1st conditional)

2 present simple, present simple (0 conditional)

3 past simple, *would* + present simple (2nd conditional)

B 1 requested
2 includes
3 would … offer
4 will receive
5 occupy
6 will / 'll be able to
7 will / 'll give
8 doubled
9 will / 'll offer

Listening 3

1 B 2 B 3 A
4 B

Review Test 3
Units 7–9

Listening Test

PART 1

1 D 2 A 3 B 4 D

PART 2

5 C 6 B 7 B 8 A
9 C 10 C 11 A 12 A
13 C

PART 3

14 A 15 C 16 C 17 B
18 C 19 C

PART 4

20 C 21 C 22 D 23 B
24 D 25 B

Reading Test

PART 5

26 D 27 C 28 C 29 D
30 D 31 A 32 B 33 C
34 C 35 B 36 B 37 D

PART 6

38 C 39 D 40 C 41 A

PART 7

42 D 43 A 44 C 45 C
46 A 47 D 48 C 49 B
50 C

Unit 10 Environment

Snapshot

A (suggested answers)

1 cattle, field, refinery, farmland, flame, smoke

2 house, balcony, window, rooftop, wall, story, facade

3 skyscraper, freeway, traffic, vehicle, building

4 cottage, coast, coastline, shore, sea, wave

B Statements B, C, E and H are accurate.

TOEIC® Tip
Words referred to in different contexts are:
A coast
D high-rise buildings
G laundry, balcony

Listening 1

B 2 bright sunshine
4 overcast skies
1 sunny intervals with scattered showers
5 heavy rain
6 fog
3 thunderstorms
9 strong winds
7 moderate snowfall
8 high pressure
10 mild temperatures

C

Germany / France	5	heavy rain
the Swiss Alps	7	snow
London	10	46°
Western Austria	9	strong winds
Spain and Portugal	8	high pressure
the Mediterranean	2	bright sunshine
the Black Sea	3	thunderstorms

Grammar Check 1

C 1 said
2 asked
3 would
4 told
5 to say
6 told
7 saying
8 had

Viewpoint

B 1 global warming
2 urban areas
3 road transportation
4 carbon emissions
5 new technologies
6 air pollution
7 parking lots
8 Recent research
9 traffic accidents
10 physical exercise

C 1 wind turbines – new technologies – urban design – parks
2 air pollution – clogged roads – deteriorating neighborhoods – traffic accidents – illness

D 1 up to 1 million
2 China
3 carbon emissions could exceed 1 billion tons
4 Curitiba

Grammar Check 2

Type a: admit to, (dis)agree with, apologize for, complain about
Type b: promise, advise, (dis)agree, claim, instruct, invite,
Type c: admit, promise, advise, (dis)agree, announce, claim, complain, confirm, propose, predict, warn

Listening 2

1 The man warned that the bus drivers would go on strike.
2 The woman invited the man to join the car pool.
3 The man advised the woman to take some warm clothing.
4 The woman apologized for changing the appointment.

Vocabulary Builder

A 1 make
2 do
3 do
4 make
5 do (carry out) / make (create)
6 make
7 do
8 make
9 do or make a deal / do business
10 make
11 make
12 make

B 1 make … change
2 making use
3 do … work
4 make … easy / possible
5 doing … housework / cooking / ironing
6 doing … programming
7 do … rest
8 doing … damage
9 do … shopping
10 make … most
11 made … miscalculations / mistakes / errors

Listening 3

A 1 When
2 What
3 How much / What
4 What
5 Which / How many
6 How
7 What
8 How many

B 1 B   2 G   3 F
4 H   5 C   6 D
7 E   8 A

Unit 11 Health

Snapshot

A (suggested answers)
1 holding, sitting, standing, placing
2 clutching, holding, standing, handing
3 balancing, standing, lifting
4 lying down, kneeling, stretching, bending, holding, lifting, bracing

1 The patient is sitting in the examination room.
The doctor is holding a stethoscope to the patient's chest.
He's standing next to the patient.

2 The worker is handing her some food.
She is holding / clutching / carrying the food.

3 They're balancing on one leg.
They're standing in a field.
They're raising their arms.
They're lifting one leg.
They're stretching out their arms.

4 The man is lying on the mat.
The man's arms are folded behind his head.

The therapist is kneeling next to him.
The therapist is stretching the patient's leg.
He's holding / lifting / bracing the man's leg.

B 1 F   2 H   3 E
4 B

Grammar Check 1

A 1 *involve* – gerund
2 *plan* – infinitive

B 1 playing
2 to attend
3 becoming
4 taking
5 being
6 to join
7 to work out
8 waiting
9 to sign
10 to extend
11 hearing
12 to contact

TOEIC® tip
1 without having to
2 of receiving
3 to hearing

Listening 1

B 1 check-up, cleaning, molars, chew, X-ray: *dentist, patient, dentist's office*
2 complete physical, see a doctor, check-up: *doctor, patient, doctor's office*
3 prescription filled, medicine, drugs, prescribed: *pharmacist, customer, pharmacy*
4 corrective lenses, eyesight, prescription, vision, read: *eye doctor / optometrist, patient*
5 health insurance benefits package, medical and dental coverage, policy, reimburses, doctor-prescribed medications: *health insurance advisor, employee, in a company office*

Viewpoint

A (suggested answers)

exercise, diet, sleep, relaxation, stimulation, hobbies, security, family

B 1 i wrong – <u>low</u> levels of cholesterol

2 i wrong – tofu (bean curd), pork
3 ii wrong – <u>more</u> stressful
iii wrong – <u>less</u> exercise
4 (suggested answers)
i doctors and the government are encouraging people to return to the traditional lifestyle
ii the local newspaper is providing advice for healthier living
iii schools are serving and teaching children about traditional foods

Listening 2

1 authors   2 recipes
3 community center   4 6 p.m.
5 9 p.m.   6 40

Grammar Check 2

A 1 first part: past perfect – second part: conditional perfect
2 first part: conditional perfect – second part: past perfect

B 1 had lived
2 wouldn't have had
3 wouldn't have been able
4 would have had
5 would have done
6 would have worked
7 wouldn't have been

Listening 3

I A   II C   III B
IV E   V D

Vocabulary Builder

1 e   2 f   3 a
4 d   5 c   6 b

Unit 12 Society

Snapshot

A (suggested answers)
1 People are attending a court session outdoors.
2 People are registering to vote in a polling station.
3 Young students are attending school.
4 Two police officers are on bicycle patrol near a market.

B 1 E, J   2 D, H   3 I, L
4 B, K

Grammar Check 1

A (suggested answers)

1 but, in spite of, *although*, despite, even though, *whereas*, yet
2 in spite of, *despite*
3 but, *however*, yet

B 1 *Even though* the new candidate has less experience, I've decided to vote for her.
2 Some people like to vote in person, *whereas* others prefer using an absentee ballot.
3 *Despite* (the) many observers monitoring the elections, there was widespread corruption.
Other contrast words: (1) Although (2) while (3) In spite of

C 1 even though
2 Even if
3 however
4 Although
5 whereas

Listening 1

A (suggested answers)

voting – polling place
educating people – classroom
law-making and governing people – city hall / capitol building
enforcing laws – courtroom, police station
reporting income and paying taxes – taxation bureau

B (suggested answers)

voting – vote, ballot, ballot box, list of candidates, voter registration, registration card
educating people – school, college, university, students, teachers, instructors, professors
law-making and governing people – legislation, rules, laws, regulations, ordinance
enforcing laws – courts, judges, lawyers, defendants, prosecutors, police, sheriff, federal agents, soldiers, military, army, navy
reporting income and paying taxes – tax forms, to file taxes, income tax, sales tax, payments, deductions

C 1 voting: register, eligible to vote, elections, voter registration card, polling place
2 enforcing laws: driver's license, vehicle registration, officer, speeding, pulled over
3 reporting income and paying taxes: filling out, income tax returns, due, to file
4 governing people: elected, in office, mayor, city, raise local taxes
5 educating people: course catalog, semester, classes, credits, MBA, university

Vocabulary Builder

A 1 d   2 a   3 f
4 e   5 c   6 b

B 1 b   2 c   3 a

C 1 highly unlikely
2 hugely successful
3 close collaboration
4 valuable lessons
5 positive attitude
6 Critically acclaimed
7 significant contribution

Listening 2

B 1 general
2 general
3 specific

C 1 d
2 b
3 c

Grammar Check 2

1 reside
2 speak
3 understand
4 be
5 show / demonstrate
6 show / demonstrate

Viewpoint

1 Freedom to decide.
2 For: it's like the real world.
Against: it's costly for the players who have been eliminated.
3 Subscribers would be dissatisfied.
4 They make decisions about the virtual world, its laws and how they are enforced.

Listening 3

A 1 disagreeing
2 asking for an opinion
3 presenting an argument
4 agreeing
5 requesting clarification

B 1 B
2 A
3 A
4 B

Review Test 4
Units 10–12

Listening Test

PART 1

1 D   2 A   3 B
4 C

PART 2

5 C   6 B   7 B
8 B   9 C   10 A
11 B   12 A   13 B
14 A

PART 3

15 D   16 A   17 C
18 C   19 B   20 A

PART 4

21 B   22 C   23 D
24 D   25 A   26 C

Reading Test

PART 5

27 D   28 C   29 C
30 A   31 C   32 B
33 D   34 A   35 B
36 C   37 C   38 C

PART 6

39 A   40 C   41 A
42 C

PART 7

43 D   44 B   45 C
46 B   47 C   48 D
49 B   50 C

Communication File

1 Careers

Role cards for temporary work agency interviews

Director of PeoplePower, Interviewer

You are one of the co-directors of PeoplePower. Your job is to choose the top performers in many different fields.

Prepare a short list of questions about the candidate's profession, skills, job functions, and experience.

PeoplePower Candidate, Interviewee

Choose a profession which you know well or one you can do some research on. In order to be listed by PeoplePower, you must convince them that you are highly motivated and well-qualified.

Prepare a short description of your profession, your skills and qualifications. What questions will you ask your potential employer?

2 Workplaces

ACTIVE PRACTICE

Student A

Describe the position of the objects to your partner. How many differences can you find?

Role cards for safety screening

Sales Representative of 'VideoScan'

You are hoping to get the contract with the Franklin Institute to supply surveillance technology. Your arguments are:
- your customers (private companies and government institutions) are very satisfied with the results of the technology – reduction of workplace misconduct and intrusions
- increased security is a must for all organizations in today's unstable society
- your company will provide technical support and training for staff in how to use the equipment appropriately
- cameras can be installed in plain view or hidden

Vice President of the Franklin Institute

You are worried that the Institute may be held responsible in the event of serious injury to a student or staff member. Your arguments in favor of CCTV (closed-circuit TV) are:
- it will be cheaper than hiring extra security staff
- unsafe areas like the underground parking lot and parts of the campus grounds can be secured
- the security services will be able to react immediately in any emergency
- video records can provide evidence in case of litigation

Professor of Psychology

You are opposed to the use of surveillance technology for the following reasons:
- there is no proof that surveillance technology changes people's behavior
- it will have a negative effect on both student and staff morale, generate stress, and make both students and staff uncomfortable
- it is an invasion of individual privacy
- it could be used to victimize certain individuals
- the Institute is an educational environment in which freedom of expression should be encouraged, not controlled

Role cards for safety screening

Student Representative

You have received reports from students concerning the theft of various personal items (laptop computers, cell phones). However, you are not sure that video surveillance equipment is necessarily a good thing. You would like to know:
- how the technology will be used and by whom
- where cameras will be installed
- whether the police will be informed of security incidents

Administration Spokesperson

You are the union representative. The union members are worried about the plan to introduce surveillance technology. Your concerns:
- the cost (it might be better to spend the money on hiring extra security personnel)
- the potential abuse of the system which could be used to monitor employee performance at work
- cameras might be hidden
- this is the first step towards more widespread surveillance (i.e. monitoring the use of computers and the telephone)

Student B

Describe the position of the objects to your partner. How many differences can you find?

3 Communications

Role cards for press conference

GloTelCom President

- You must announce that GloTelCom is laying off 2,000 workers because of poor financial results.
- GloTelCom would like to continue to operate in the local community.
- Avoid journalists' questions about whether GloTelCom will move operations overseas. It is true that GloTelCom is considering moving its operations, but you do not want to discuss this now.

GloTelCom Spokesperson

- The layoffs are only temporary. GloTelCom supports its workers.
- You will explain the benefit packages being given to laid-off employees.
- Each worker will receive:
  - three months' additional salary (severance pay)
  - six months' health insurance coverage.

The Mayor

- You are afraid the layoffs will greatly affect the local economy and damage your chances of being re-elected, so you want to reassure the public.
- You will announce that the government is working with GloTelCom to create more job opportunities.

Employee Union Representative

- The GloTelCom layoff package is not enough.
- The laid-off workers should receive:
  - six months' salary as severance pay
  - one year of health insurance coverage
  - GloTelCom should pay for re-training and educational programs.
- You should ask whether GloTelCom plans to close its operations in the area.

Journalist

- You want to know the real reasons for the layoffs. Are they going to close both local plants permanently?
- GloTelCom has been conducting negotiations with manufacturers overseas.
- The CEO has made four trips overseas in the last six months. Why?
- Ask the mayor why he/she said two weeks ago that the local job market was "strong and stable".

4 Retailing

Role cards for presenting a product

Card A

The IceMaker
An elegant, compact kitchen appliance to produce ice cubes!

Capacity   produces 40 small, medium or large ice cubes every hour

Cost   350 U.S. dollars

Card B

Safe Bather
A battery-powered alarm system that lets you know when your bath tub is full – before it's too late!

Cost   25 U.S. dollars

Card C

KeyLocator
A discreet, programmable battery-operated key ring that allows you to find those lost keys. Just dial your KeyLocator number on your cell phone and your KeyLocator key ring will respond with a ringing tone.

Cost   299 U.S. dollars

Card D

CorkMaestro
An all-electric corkscrew that takes the work out of opening bottles. Your guests will be amazed!

Cost   98 U.S. dollars

5 Industry

Role cards for construction and development versus preservation and heritage

Land Developer

You have invested a lot of money in the industrial park. Your project will provide much-needed manufacturing and office space for businesses, bringing income into the community.

You want a guarantee from the mayor that construction will continue in three months.

Construction Superintendent

Your concern is the construction schedule, which cannot stop.

You have many sub-contractors working on the project and delays will be costly.

You want to continue working in areas away from the excavations.

Mayor

On the one hand, the new industrial park will be beneficial to local business.

On the other hand, the preservation of historical sites will bring in tourism.

You will have to make the final decision about the site.

Archeologist

All construction must stop while your teams survey the entire site.

You will need a minimum of eight months and full access to the entire construction site.

Ideally you would like to have a full fourteen months.

President of the Local Heritage Foundation

All construction on the industrial complex must permanently stop.

The government should purchase the site to create a museum and cultural heritage center.

The museum would bring in many tourists and help the local economy.

Tourism will attract more businesses.

6 Trade

Role cards for fair trade or free trade?

Store Manager

You have serious doubts about the Fairtrade Town initiative. You believe that:

- there is no proof that guaranteeing a fixed price for goods promotes economic prosperity
- free market prices determined by supply and demand are better than promoting the interests of producers and consumers
- the initiative would only be interesting if it boosts business activity in the community

President of the Local Farmers' Union

You represent a small group of local farmers. You believe that:
- promoting Fairtrade products would be at the expense of locally grown produce
- the local agricultural industry could suffer as a result
- your organization could only support the Fairtrade initiative if it also promotes local products

Town Council Member

You have organized this meeting in response to a petition in favor of becoming a Fairtrade Town. As the chairperson for the meeting, you should present the agenda and act as the moderator for the discussion. You are interested in hearing all opinions but you believe that:
- you may not have the budget to support this initiative
- it could hurt the local business community
- it could enhance the town's image

Fairtrade Spokesperson

You are actively promoting the Fairtrade initiative and have assisted other communities in adopting it. Your experience has shown that:
- Fairtrade is a growth sector (+ 30%) over the last two years
- Fairtrade can improve the community image
- it can promote community cohesion and development
- it develops public awareness of global trade issues

Consumer Group Representative

You are a member of a local consumer group. You believe that:
- consumers' views are often ignored by retailers
- Fairtrade is a growing market
- Fairtrade ultimately benefits the consumer by improving the quality and the choice of goods available

7 Leisure

Sailing

Accompanied by a sea captain, the group will spend two days sailing on a yacht. On the first morning, the group will learn basic sailing techniques and receive Level I National Sailing Associations Certification. The second day will end with a regatta.
Two-day rates start at €400 per person.

Deep Sea Fishing

The group will be taken fifteen miles offshore to fish for tuna, halibut, and shark. The 48' fully-equipped boat has overnight capacity so that the trip can range from eight to 24 hours.
Cost: €1,600 for a full day or € 2,400 for two days and a night.

Cooking

Enjoy cooking classes, gourmet meals, and a night in a luxury hotel. You will work with our top chefs to prepare a seven-course dinner for the group.
Cost is: €400 per person, food and accommodation included.

Survival School

The group will participate in a three-day survival school. Outdoor survival lessons include building overnight shelters, preparing meals in the outdoors, and administering emergency first aid.
Cost: €500 per person for three days.

Race-Car Driving

Your group will be taken to the Motor Speedway and given instruction on race-car driving. Afterwards you will practice driving cars that reach speeds of up to 220 kilometers per hour and participate in a real race.
Cost: €300 per person for a day trip including lunch.

9 Travel

Role cards for eco-tourism development

Local Community Leader

Visitors should be limited to 30 people per month.
Eco-tourism developers must make a ten-year commitment to the project.
Profits should be divided as follows:
- 50% should be given to the local community
- 20% should be re-invested in developing tourist programs and facilities
- 30% should go to non-local shareholders and investors

Eco-tourism Developer

You would like to bring in ten groups of six people every month.
You will commit to a six-year contract.
Profits should be divided as follows:
- You and your company should receive 30%
- 30% to the local community
- 30% to the shareholders
- 10% to the local Non-Governmental Organization who will oversee the sustainable development

Eco-tourism Financial Investor

You would like to bring in 100 eco-tourists every month.
You would like to limit the initial contract to three years.
Profits should be divided as follows:
- You expect to receive 60%
- 20% to local individuals who work for the eco-tourism project
- 20% for the eco-tourism developers

NGO Representative

Limit the number of visitors to 30 per month.
The contract's minimum duration should be ten to twelve years.
Profits should be divided as follows:
- 30% should be given to the local leaders
- 15% to the locals working on the project
- 25% to the investors and shareholders
- 15% to the eco-tourism developers
- 10% to federal government officials
- 5% should be donated to local Non-Governmental Organizations

10 Environment

Role cards for winds of change

Spokesperson for Wind Gen, the group of electricity companies

You represent the companies who are planning to build the offshore wind towers. Your group will be making a huge investment, as the project is expected to cost 700–800 million dollars. You are convinced that the development is in the best interests of both the local community and the state as a whole. Among the arguments that you can use are:
- the project will reduce pollution
- it will ultimately provide enough electricity for 100,000 homes
- it will create jobs and position Cape Cod as a leader in the use of alternative power sources
- it will reduce the state's requirements for natural gas

Spokesperson for New England Maritime Commission, the authority for local maritime affairs

You represent the various maritime authorities and the local fishermen. You are opposed to the project for the following reasons:
- the development represents a collision danger for shipping (particularly passenger ferries)
- construction of wind towers could change the pattern of currents and lead to the creation of new uncharted sandbanks
- local fishermen may be excluded from the 24-square-mile area. Cables will also have to be laid between the towers and the shore and may constitute a hazard for fishermen

Spokesperson for Cape Cod Community Watch, local residents' committee

Your association seeks to defend the environment of Cape Cod as it is now. You are opposed to industrial development even if it is to provide alternative energy. Your reasons are:

- the towers, which are 250 feet tall, will be visible from coastal towns and will detract from the natural beauty of the Cape
- the development could have negative effects on marine mammals and on the migratory birds that visit the area
- tourism may be adversely affected and real estate may lose value
- there is a danger of pollution from lubricating oil that is contained in the towers
- the forecast energy production figures may be exaggerated
- turbine noise may be carried downwind toward the land

Spokesman for AltaVolta, the alternative energy lobby

Your association promotes the use of alternative energy sources. You believe this is an opportunity to oppose current policies which favor generating electricity by burning fossil fuels. Your main arguments are:

- the forecasts show that demand for electricity in the area will grow
- Cape Cod is ideally situated to benefit from abundant wind power
- wind power will lead to greater decentralization of electricity production
- the planned project will lead to better quality of life for Cape Cod residents
- wind power is clean, efficient and renewable
- the project is a test case for environmental protection and could lead to positive changes in national energy policy

11 Health

Role cards for keeping the company healthy

Card A

You are studying how the company's headquarters can be redesigned to encourage employees to get more exercise. Your suggestions are:

- relocate the parking areas so that employees will have to walk further
- widen and decorate existing stairways to make them more attractive to use
- relocate the company cafeteria outside the main company building
- install smaller, slower elevators

Card B

You are looking into how to set up an on-site company fitness center where employees would be able to work out during office hours. Your recommendations are:

- the center should be staffed by professionals
- each employee should draw up a personal fitness plan
- employees who achieve their personal goals will receive a bonus
- medical consultations will be given free of charge
- quiet rooms will be available for employees to relax in

Card C

You are analyzing the benefits of giving staff individual health assessments. You would like to introduce:

- a voluntary program of health risk assessment – staff will receive the results of a medical examination
- free counselling
- a weekly seminar on healthy living
- an internal website with advice and guidelines
- a 24-hour health hotline

Card D

You are evaluating ways of promoting better health and hygiene for the staff. You believe the company should:

- introduce a strict no-smoking policy – only non-smokers will be recruited, and anyone found smoking at work will be dismissed
- remove all vending machines that sell soda-based drinks and confectionery and supply only water fountains
- eliminate high-calorie foods from the cafeteria menu
- purchase special office furniture for all computer users

12 Society

Debate: Should avatars in virtual worlds have the power to "eliminate" other players?

Group A

Arguments FOR
Virtual worlds should be as realistic as possible. Most players prefer power. Avatars should be able to do anything they want. Virtual violence doesn't hurt anyone. Virtual worlds should be a place where players can act out aggressions. The real world is safer if people can act out their aggressions in virtual worlds. People are free to leave the virtual world whenever they want to.

Group B

Arguments AGAINST
Virtual worlds should reflect human ideals not reality. Humans desire equality. Avatars should be empowered for good and not bad. Virtual violence is still a type of violence – psychological and moral. Virtual worlds should be where people can realize their dreams and actualize their ideals. Virtual violence promotes violence in the real world. Virtual worlds should be hospitable and inviting places for new members.

Acknowledgements

The authors would like to express their sincere and heartfelt thanks to the following people for their assistance and encouragement during the research and writing of *Target Score*.

- The Cambridge University Press editorial team, with special thanks to Susan Power, Content Editor, First Edition, Tracy Allerton, Content Editor, Second Edition, and Sally Searby, Publishing Manager, for their expert guidance and advice at all stages of the project. Thanks to Sophie Clarke for managing the project through production and thanks too to our Copyeditors, Annie Cornford, Catriona Watson-Brown and Alison Silver, and Photo Researcher, Sandie Huskinson-Rolfe.
- The team at Cambridge University Press for their assistance and support: Gary Anderson, Sam Dumiak, Terry Elliott, Angela Lilley, Clare MacCallum, Gemma Wilkins, Vivien Tweed, and Marie Allan.
- Our colleagues and students at The American University of Paris and at the Université de Paris XII. Particular thanks to Laurence Baierlein and Wayne Drexler.

We would also like to extend our thanks to the following people who contributed in important ways to the success of the project: Brenda Turnnidge, Bernie Hayden, Kate Franzmann, Laurence Gouttefangeas, Emilia Sofia, Lucy Allardyce, Fiona Inguih, Valerie Grauer, Emma Hilton, Frances Kan, Laura Mackinnon, Yvonne Raemdonck, Clive Skinner.

And last, but not least, many thanks to our families and friends.

The authors and publishers are grateful to the following for permission to reproduce copyright material. It has not always been possible to identify the source of material used or to contact the copyright holders and in such cases the publishers would welcome information from the copyright owners. *The New York Times*, for the article on p. 13, 'Indian Companies are Adding Western Flavor' by Saritha Rai, 19 August 2003, for the article on p. 58 , 'Juan Valdez brews up a plan', 29 November 2003, for the article on p. 82, adapted from 'The Rising Value of Play Money', by Amy Wu, 1 February 2004, and for the article on p. 90., 'Exotic Trips for Eco-tourists' by Martha Stevenson Olson, 10 March 2002, © The New York Times Company; reprinted with permission; *South Florida Sun-Sentinel*, 27 August 2002 for the article on p. 23, 'Little Brother sees into your cubicle' by Joan Fleischer Tamen, reprinted with permission from the South Florida Sun-Sentinel; for the extracts and photos on pp. 42-43 from Camper website (www.camper.es), reprinted with permission from Camper; for the logo, photos and adapted text on pp. 48-49 from the Jelly Belly website virtual tour (www.jellybelly.com), © Jelly Belly ® Candy Company; for the Café de Colombia logo on p. 58, by permission of the National Federation of Coffee Growers of Colombia; for the Fairtrade logo on p. 62, by permission of the Fairtrade Foundation; for the texts on p. 70 from the Leisure Trends website (www.leisuretrends.com), © Leisuretrends.com; for the extract on p. 72 from 'Drive-in cinema is Norway's coolest' by Lars Bevanger, 6 April 2004; © the BBC News website; Australian Bureau of Statistics for the table on p. 78, 'Changing Composition of Household Income' from Household Income, Table 2, Catalogue No. 1301.0. Published in the Year Book Australia 2001, 25 January 2001. ABS data used with permission from the Australian Bureau of Statistics (www.abs.gov.au); for the tables on p. 79 ,'Consumer Prices'. Used with permission of the Bureau of Labor Statistics; for the extract on p. 102 , adapted from 'Curbing Sprawl to Fight Climate Change'. Used with permission of the Worldwatch Institute; *Newsweek*; adapted from 'The Okinawa Way' by Hideko Takayama, 6 May 2004, © 2004 Newsweek, Inc. All rights reserved. Reprinted by permission. Dan Hunter and F Gregory Lastowka for the article on p. 121, 'To Kill an Avatar', published in *Legal Affairs*, July–August 2003.

The TOEIC® test directions are reprinted by permission of Educational Testing Service. However, the test questions and any other testing information are provided by Cambridge University Press. No endorsement of this publication by Educational Testing Service should be inferred.

Photo Acknowledgements

t = top, b = bottom, l = left, r = right, m = middle

Acestock.com: p.123bl; Copyright ADP/J Burlot: p.10bl; © lookGaleria/Alamy: p.32; ©Eddie Gerald/Alamy: p.69tl, ©ChrisWillson/Alamy: p.110, © Marc Romanelli/Alamy: p.114; Under the Pergola at Naples, 1914 by Boccioni, Umberto (1882-1916), Civica Galleria d'Arte, Moderna, Milan, Italy/Bridgeman: p.56tl, Blue and White bowl painted with Chinese characters, Longqing Mark and period (1567-72) (porcelain), by Chinese School (16th century), Private Collection/Bridgeman: p.56bl, Baga D'mba Mask, Guinea (wood), by African Private Collection, ©Heini Schneebeli/Bridgeman: p.56br; Camera Press London: p.72; ©Vittoriano Rastelli/Corbis: p.10tl, ©Paul Barton/Corbis: pp.11 & 107tl, ©Francis G Mayer/Corbis: p.12(1), ©Bettmann/Corbis: p.12(2), ©Petre Buzoianu/Corbis: p.12(5), © Layne Kennedy/Corbis: p.33tl, ©Douglas Kirkland/Corbis: p.33tr, © Henry Diltz/Corbis: p.33br, ©Gail Mooney/Corbis: p.39tl, ©Pablo Corral/Corbis: p.39tr, ©Keith Dannemiller/Corbis: p.39bl, ©Viviane Moos/Corbis: p.39br, ©Steve Raymer/Corbis: p.47tl, ©Roger Ball/Corbis: p.47br, ©Lindsay Hebberd/Corbis: p.55tl, ©Kelly-Mooney/Corbis: p.55br, ©Jodice Mimmo/Corbis: p.56tr, ©Jon Feingersh/zefa/Corbis: p.60, ©Peter Johnson/Corbis: p.69bl, ©Philip Gould/Corbis: p.69br, ©Bohemian Nomad Picturemakers/Corbis: p.77tr, ©Reza; Webistan/Corbis: p.77bl, ©Reuters/Corbis: pp.52, 85tl, ©Henry Romero/Reuters/Corbis: p.85br, ©Roger de la Harpe/Corbis: p.90, ©Michael S Yamashita/Corbis: p.93tl, ©Dennis Degnan/Corbis: p.99tr, ©Michael St. Maur Sheil/Corbis: p.99br, ©Buddy Mays/Corbis: p.104, ©Ed Quinn/Corbis: p.106t, ©Royalty Free/Corbis: pp.107bl & br, ©Karl Weatherly/Corbis: p.115br, ©Julien Hekimian/Corbis Sygma: p.9tl, ©Timothy Fadek/Corbis Sygma: p.9tr, ©Colin McPherson/Corbis Sygma: p.12(6), ©Patrick Durand/Corbis Sygma: p.25tr, ©Sion Touhig/Corbis Sygma: p.55tr; Photograph by Kate Crozier, photographersdirect.com: p.9br; 'CTK/Sovfoto', photographersdirect.com: p.93tr; Kayte Deioma Photography, photographersdirect.com: p.25br; Getty Images: pp.12(3), 12(4), 12(7), 17tl, bl & br, 45, 47tr & bl, 52 background, 55bl, 63tl, tr, bl & br, 69tr, 85tr & bl, 86 all, 94l & r, 99tl, 100t, 115tr; Paul Glendell, photographersdirect.com: p.106b; Photo courtesy IBM, used with kind permission: p.18; Camper Foodball Restaurant, Concept: Marti Guixé, foto: Imagekontainer, Barcelona 2004: p.42r; istockphoto.com: pp.46l & br, 58, 70tl & bl; Chris King: p.84; Patricia Lanza Photography, photographersdirect.com: p.10br; LEC: p.46tr; Contessa Ice Machine, photo courtesy Syd Lloyd: p.46bl; ©Dan McCoy/Rainbow, photographersdirect.com: p.17tr; Mike Goldwater/Network: p.9bl, Sion Touhia/Network: p.73; Nikhilesh Havel (nikreations@yahoo.com), photographersdirect.com: p.70tm; George Oze Photography, photographersdirect.com: p.119; ©Paul Quayle/Panos Pictures: p.115tl, ©Jacob Silberberg/Panos Pictures: p.115bl, ©Mark Henley/Panos Pictures: p.123br; THE OKINAWA WAY: HOW TO IMPROVE YOUR HEALTH AND LONGEVITY DRAMATICALLY by Bradley J Willcox, D Craig Willcox & Makoto Suzuki, foreword Andrew Weil (Penguin General, 2001) Copyright ©Bradley J Willcox, D Craig Willcox & Makoto Suzuki, 2001. Foreword copyright ©Andrew Weil. 'Front cover reproduced by permission of Penguin Books Ltd': p.111; 'Cover design and photo' by Joseph Perez and Carolyn Bauman, photograph from LIFE IS SO GOOD by George Dawson and Richard Glaubman, copyright ©2000 by George Dawson & Richard Glaubman. Used by permission of Penguin, a division of Penguin Group (USA) Inc: p.118; Trevor Humphries/Rex Features: p.25tl, Stock Connection/Rex Features: p.33bl, Barcroft Media Ltd/Rex Features: p.105; Used with kind permission of the Rich Dad Company: p.82, Steve Sant, photographersdirect.com: p.70tr; NOAA/Science Photo Library: p.100bl, Copyright ©Geospace/Science Photo Library: p.100br; Shooting Star International, photographersdirect.com: p.25bl; Bill Bachmann/Spectrum Photofile, photographersdirect.com: p.123tl; Markus Matzel/Still Pictures: p.107tr; www.the4cs.com: p.21; Chad Ehlers/Tips Images, photographersdirect.com: p.99bl; Topfoto/Imageworks: pp. 77tl & br, 123tr; Brenda Turnnidge: p.90; 'Designed by Jacque Fresco, courtesy of The Venus Project, www.FutureByDesign.com': p.104.

Picture Research by Sandie Huskinson of PHOTOSEEKERS.

Cartoons: © 2003 The New Yorker Collection from cartoonbank.com: pages 14, 19, 28, 44, 61, 90, 109 and 117; Cartoon stock: page 83.

Illustrations: Rupert Besley, pages 15, 24, 29, 75, 103, 112 and 122; Francis Fung pages 86, 92 and 121; Tim Oliver, pages 78, 100, 106, 168 and 169; Tony Wilkins, page 20.

Cover photos: Corbis for airport, man in glasses, woman with bag and coach; Alamy for man and woman having lunch, aeroplane, road and man with briefcase.